Project Integrity
∞International

Philosophy & Plan for a New Economy

ABCrane

Gungho Publishing

Project Integrity International: Philosophy & Plan for a New Economy
ABCrane

Published by Gungho Publishing
Project Integrity International
www.projectintegrity.biz

For information about this book, visit www.projectintegrity.biz.

ISBN-13: 978-0-9789789-3-8

Copyright © 2019 Gungho Publishing
Sunnyvale, CA
Published in the United States of America

Cover layout, logos, collage art, and infographics by ABCrane
Cover artwork by Thomas Walkup © 2007

∞

In the Spirit of Individualism—
Dedicated to Each,

Within the Soul of Oneness—
Dedicated to All.

∞

Other Works By ABCrane

Learn more about these works at www.projectintegrity.biz.

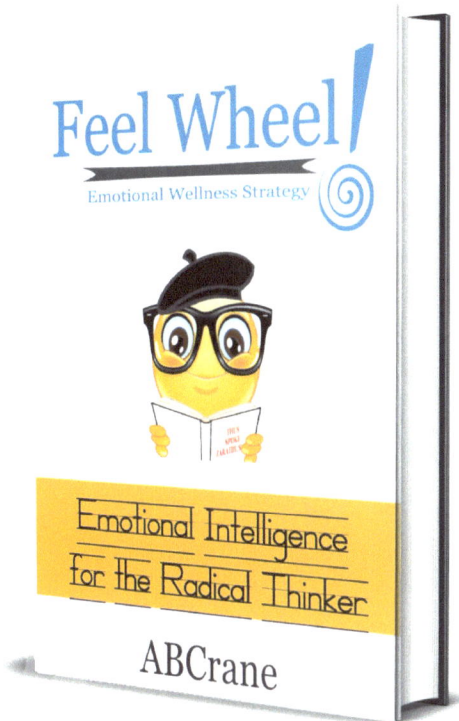

What all human beings share in common is that their emotional states play a leading role in directing the quality and productivity of their lives. For the radical thinkers among us, emotionality can often be greatly amplified in the face of our facing of reality as we plunge down the proverbial rabbit hole of deep paralyzing despair that sometimes renders us counterproductive at best and self-destructive at worst. **The Feel Wheel Emotional Wellness Strategy** is designed to help radical thinkers—and all other readers—to manage their emotions in a way that preserves the sense of self, meaningfulness, and effectiveness inherent in each and every one of us. *includes journaling worksheets, emotion quote cards, and game spinner for individual and group play*

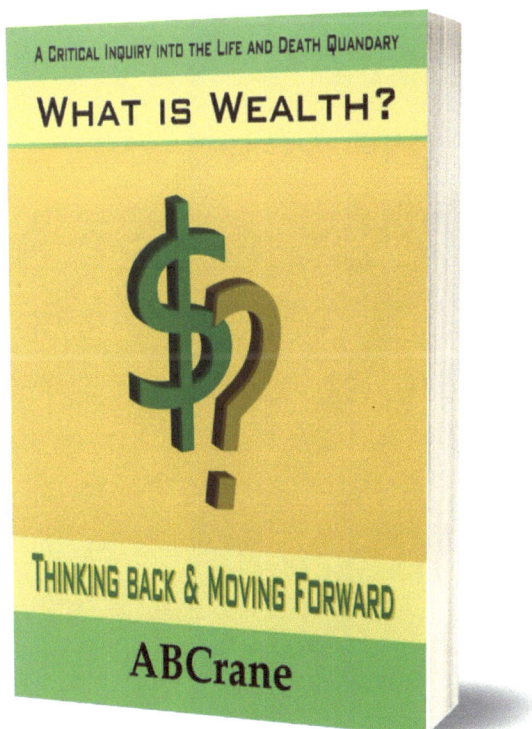

What *is Wealth?* not only addresses the myriad of ills plaguing human societies across the globe, but attempts to pinpoint their interconnected causation through a cross-disciplinary examination. The critical inquiry into the age old question, "What is Wealth?," is the starting point whereby individuals and communities can begin to innovate and implement economic models that benefit workers, consumers, and the natural environment.

CONTENTS

THE REVOLUTION OF REVOLUTION

Many great steps forward were taken in the twentieth century to address the world's epidemics. Freedom fighters, conscientious objectors, and their civilian anti-war allies organized independence movements that resisted the brutal invasion and occupation of their homelands by foreign imperialists driven by power and profit. Challenging horrific working conditions were organized laborers who demanded better wages, shorter work days, and safer workplace conditions. Civil Rights activists who battled against hundreds of years of slavery, racism, and discrimination began to achieve greater social and economic status. Chiseling away at millennia of male subjugation, misogyny, and unequal treatment were women who called out for equal status and rights. Psychologists, sociologists, social workers, and others challenged child abuse and domestic violence while environmentalists rejected the toxic lifestyle of addiction-driven consumerism that depletes rain forests, the ozone layer, and fresh water. Seeking alternatives to both fundamental religion and secular materialistic lifestyles, both of which left little room for creative expression and individuality, were spiritualists who dared to stretch their consciousness beyond the status quo way of life. Entrepreneurs started sustainable businesses and charitable non-profits that fostered social justice and a healthier environment. Millions of people throughout the world made great changes. Despite reactionary governments, greedy corporations, and mass indifference, the progress fortunately continues.

Today more than ever, we must accelerate these critical changes. Our current global economic systems are failing to safely and affordably feed, clothe, house, transport, and educate the world's population. Obesity gobbles down toxic treats as famine scrambles for a few grains of rice. Privilege speeds by in fancy sports cars, while poverty cups her hands hoping to score some spare change. Public transportation systems deteriorate beneath a melting sky as governments dole out welfare to wealthy automobile corporations. The economic imbalance between individuals, sexes, races, and nations is all too apparent on every street corner, in every town, and in every nation. As consumerism—the new global culture of shop-'til-you-drop—rampantly spreads across the planet, so do pollution, labor abuses, and human misery. Landfills overflow while rivers dry up. The automobile industry expands along with the hole in the ozone. Wars are waged in the great rush for more and more, while acres of rain forests become less and less. Pop culture replaces all others as the masses turn to an excess of junk food, alcohol, television, and drugs to fill in the void.

People lurking on the edges of society try to bring sense and harmony to a crazy war-torn world. These souls traipse through the darkness, spreading light where illumination is desperately needed. The voice cries out for peace, truth, wisdom, harmony—justice! Some shout it in the streets, while others stream it online. But as the poignant progressive voice bellows out from between the creases of cyber space and Roman time, something shifts ever so slightly within the frequency of my perceptive faculties. The voice, still powerfully profound in its ideas and sentiments, now fails to grab hold of my mind and spirit as it once so has. Yes, the truth still rings true—and the epidemics still clutter the landscape of so-called Democracy.

But a quiet epiphany reveals itself in profound whispers. A new kind of progressive. A revolution of revolution. The ideas, epidemics, and sentiments of the progressive ideology still reflect the same in the mirror of truth, but the light in the mirror begins to refract at that trajectory where problem meets solution.

The traditional progressive movement has focussed its efforts, resources, and manpower on countless nonprofits, nonviolent resistance, consumer boycotts, worker strikes, and charitable drives. The anti-corporate movement has taken front and center stage in the saga of justice, shedding light on environmental, consumer, and labor abuses committed by many large companies across the globe.

Perhaps the greatest conundrum perplexing the progressive movement lies in this anti/pro-corporate debate. The corporate world provides the majority of our jobs, consumer products, and luxuries that comprise the lifestyle that we have grown accustomed to since the dawn of the Industrial Revolution and subsequent Information Age. Despite obvious and prolific corporate abuses, our survival has become directly contingent upon many of the products, services, and jobs provided by corporate entities across the globe.

Where these corporations leave off, many nonprofits start up, attempting to either undo damage to labor bodies and the natural environment; or by picking up the slack of corporations that fail to adequately provide for basic needs and a livable income. Many focus on providing direct charities to low income persons, while others provide job training and affordable education to such underserved groups within the greater demographic.

Still, the corporate military-industrial dominated world continues to triumph despite countless "nonprofit sector" attempts to feed the hungry, employ the jobless, and otherwise help the helpless. **It is at this trajectory, that crossing point between status quo driven global epidemics and status quo global "solutions" where the light in the mirror of my mind's eye begins to sharply refract. It is at this very juncture where the truth is revealed in the mirror: that, while many terrific solutions have been implemented by incredible people to help combat a myriad of social ills across the globe, the paradigm itself has never truly changed.** Worker strikes drive corporations to outsource domestic jobs to foreign countries. Numerous nonprofit organizations are modeled on for-profit corporations with top-heavy bureaucracies and highly paid directors, often with little charity left over for the intended recipients. Charities that assist people with job training and education prepare the next corporate work force that led to gross economic inequalities in the first place. And although many of these organizations raise awareness of so many issues, the mainstream media chimes out at a much higher decibel than fringe podcasts and progressive radio stations morse coding the globe.

How many anti-corporate protests will we march sporting shoes, t-shirts, jeans, and accessories provided by and purchased from such companies? Anti-corporate activists like to point to the very structure of the corporate legal entity as being the root cause of modern day secular evils. Anti-corporate proponents argue that the "corporate personhood" and Limited Liability aspects of the legal entity itself allow for corporations to commit environmental, consumer, and labor abuses without consequence. But if we can see the basic legal entity as an empty bowl, we can begin to realize that it is not the bowl but its contents that bring about pollution and abuse. If we fill the bowl with products, services, advertisements, and marketing strategies that deliberately manipulate our addictive tendencies, emotional vulnerability, and instinctual impulses, the bowl becomes as toxic as its contents. On the other hand, if we fill that same bowl—the corporate legal entity that allows for limited liability and so-called personhood—with green products, healthy lifestyle marketing, and "be your own boss" entrepreneurial opportunities in the sustainable market place—we can begin to actually take advantage of that limited liability and corporate personhood towards the maximization of our efforts.

An effort in this direction can be seen as a Middle Way Solution for World Economic Success. Not only do people begin to access what they need immediately to survive in a holistic, healthy way, but the paradigm itself changes altogether. The push and pull between the world of corporate dominance and nonprofit philanthropy transforms into a world where new independent, sustainable enterprises gradually replace existing, toxic military industrial entities—but too, greatly diminishes the need for charity itself. In the new paradigm, beggars become buyers, corporate employees become independent entrepreneurs, and coworkers, supervisors, and managers simply become startup partners. The Mother Company is a corporation—a People's Corporation—and merely functions to consolidate, and thus reduce, redundant bureaucratic activity while protecting the liability of individual companies. It is the Middle Way, the way of moderation—a fluid catalyst moderating between two warring polarized ideologies. It is the same bowl, filling with the pure elements of common decency, common sense, and common cause. A Middle Way, taking front and center stage in a healthy world with countless opportunities and endless possibilities. A world, not perfect—but perfectly progressing.

By providing an economic platform that welcomes individuals from all personal backgrounds and professional disciplines, Project Integrity International will support the technological, ecological, human rights, multicultural, and spiritual movements brewing today throughout the world. PII will foster a healthier world by more intelligently utilizing the abundant resources of Planet Earth. Because PII will shelter many individuals under one umbrella, it will strengthen the movement at large by eliminating the wastefulness of redundant bureaucratic activity and by continually re-circulating resources, capital, and profits back into its own economy. Finally, PII focuses its efforts upon creating new businesses rather than challenging or attacking existing ones. PII does not propose to violently overthrow the current government. Nor, unlike other revolutions throughout history, does it call out for a mass labor strike or for the boycott of goods and services. Thus, PII will avoid creating a social and economic environment filled with contention and contempt.

The success of PII will depend on the harmonized efforts of many individuals of all ages, races, genders, nationalities, political leanings, and professional disciplines. As an international movement, PII will evenly disperse its business entities across continents so as to maintain a critical balance of political, economic, and military power between nations. By not upsetting this critical balance, PII will be able to advance all the more smoothly and effectively across the world to accomplish its mission.

So, what are we waiting for? Why shall we suffer on state or corporate assembly lines while we can be flourishing in our own gardens and holistic shops? Why not abandon the dusty union halls and recycle the tattered old manifestos in exchange for independent businesses and collective sustainable spaces? Let each become his own man, let each be her own boss—and put an end to the infantilism we all suffer in the 9 to 5 careerist agenda of the stale old elite establishment.   We need not stay fleeing, fighting, or frozen in this age old conundrum one moment beyond now. The time has come to give birth to a fresh outlook, a more effective economic system, and an emerging era in which individuals, communities, and nations survive and thrive together. Let us collaborate to restore our sacred rain forests, to grow splendid gardens, and to build more viable infrastructures that benefit both human beings and the greater natural environment. Let us put an end to the tragic bloody struggles between sexes, races, generations, religions, political parties, classes, and nations—and begin to appreciate the beautiful differences that we all share in common. The time is now.
Project Integrity International welcomes all!

THE MISSION OF THE VISION

Project Integrity International intends to create the kind of global society that can tackle the critical issues facing humankind at the beginning of the twenty first century.

But *how*, exactly? PII proposes the plan for an international franchise of environmentally sustainable worker-owned cooperative businesses. These business enterprises will not only bring economic independence, environmental health, and critical survival necessities to their co-owners, but help to resolve the world's issues and epidemics. Unlike random small businesses, PII bridges individual cooperatives with a unique franchise model designed to provide a sturdy, structured, and well organized support system for its members.

What exactly is an "international franchise of environmentally sustainable worker-owned cooperative businesses?" The term franchise refers to the right or license that is granted to one or more individuals to market a company's goods or services in a given territory. A franchise business might be a store, restaurant, or other company that an entrepreneur owns and operates under a license agreement with the franchise founder, who in turn retains legal possession of the franchise's copyrights, trademarks, and patents. Examples of iconic modern-day franchises are McDonalds, Burger King, Gold's Gym, Blockbuster Video, and Hilton Hotels. Many successful sustainable franchises such as vegan fast food chains, eco-friendly cleaning services, and second-hand stores have cropped up in the last two decades. A chain of franchises may be small and regional, or span the entire globe. One feature that makes franchise chains successful is a strong emphasis on branding—that is, incorporating fancy logos, catchy tag lines, competitive pricing, and product uniqueness to distinguish one's products and services from others. These branding tools are used to popularize goods and services that are consistently affordable, reliable, and convenient. As a result of spreading far and wide, successful franchises are able to exploit an economy of scale that allows them to offer the most competitive pricing. By spreading internationally, PII's franchises will bridge individuals, communities, and nations that will work together to strengthen the new global economic system.

Most current franchises are characterized by traditional business hierarchies of owners, managers, supervisors, and workers. Alternatively, PII franchises will be structured as cooperatives—or businesses that are co-owned and operated by entrepreneurial team members who enjoy equal profits, decision-making power, and skill-building opportunities as earned by their collective efforts.

PII's co-op franchises will provide ecosustainable goods and services—that is, goods and services that promote the well-being of both consumers and the greater natural environment. Examples of ecosustainable products and services include alternative fuels, certified organic fruits and vegetables, and goods made out of recycled materials. Many popular franchises such as fast-food chains play on human addictions, pedaling products that are unhealthy for consumers, workers, and the greater natural environment. PII's brand name, "WISR," was chosen because it is smarter for consumers to choose products and services that promote health. Rather than manipulating people to indulge in unhealthy products and lifestyles, WISR brands will foster a socioeconomic climate that encourages consumers to make informed choices that benefit everyone.

Although millions of small businesses open across the globe every year, a majority of them fold within a short time. Five unique features of PII will foster and secure the success of WISR Franchises. First, PII's headquarters will provide training and assistance with all complicated administrative tasks. Thus, inexperienced entrepreneurs will be able to succeed without getting lost along the paper trail. Second, PII will create and utilize a series of maps to plot the locations where franchises will yield the most success, thereby eliminating the potential for business failure. Third, PII will provide an extensive training and intern program to prepare franchisees to effectively run their businesses. Fourth, PII will be a "closed economy"—that is, an economy whereby capital generated by franchises is re-circulated back into the WISR economy by encouraging franchisees to shop at other WISR stores and by granting all franchisees shares in the greater PII establishment. Finally, WISR Creations motto reads "Global Brand, Local Flavor." Unlike most global franchise chains, no two WISR Franchises will be the same. Although all franchises will distribute and sell WISR Creations retail products, franchisees will design and decorate their storefronts, market their products, and present themselves to the public in a way that is unique to their own personalities and cultural backgrounds. For example, all WISR brand restaurants will use the same high-quality, organic, fair-trade ingredients in their cuisine, but their individual menus will reflect the talents, preferences, and cultural backgrounds of individual WISR Franchisees. Like the greater natural environment, WISR Franchisees will celebrate endless, mind-inspiring diversity.

What a healthy alternative! PII will become the second home to the economically disenfranchised people of the world by welcoming all nationalities, disciplines, races, genders, age levels, and classes. Inner-city youth across the world can choose to earn a healthy living as a franchisee rather than seeking financial opportunity in gangs or the military, killing innocent bystanders and foreign civilians only to return home to suffer terrible aftereffects. Isolated housewives can reconnect to their communities and achieve economic independence by discovering their independent businesswomen within. Minimum wage and sweatshop workers who seek more meaningful jobs and higher wages can open franchises that provide endless financial and artisanal skill-building opportunities. People all over the world who find themselves bored and frustrated with their corporate careers can also make a fresh start as franchisees. Because PII is an international enterprise, citizens and residents of poor nations can open franchises that bring resources, services, and independence to their communities, neighborhoods, and nations while becoming less dependent on foreign assistance and local charity.

By its very structure, PII will deliver prosperity, equality, peace, enjoyment, and environmental health to all corners of the world. PII's WISR Cooperative Franchise opportunities will be available to anyone who puts in the effort to achieve them.

THE SIX ALIENATIONS & SIX MOVEMENTS TOWARDS REINTEGRATION

Project Integrity International bridges, organizes, and unifies six present day movements intended to alleviate six corresponding alienations troubling individuals, institutions, and communities throughout the world. Although PII is not a Marxist nor a communistic movement—**but rather a purely entrepreneurial vision**—it borrows and expands upon certain idealogical tenets from the works of Karl Marx.

In his *Economic and Philosophic Manuscripts of 1844*, Marx identifies four types of alienation experienced by laborers under a capitalist system of industrial production. PII expands on this concept by adding two more types of alienation greatly effecting workers and consumers in today's globalized economy.

Each of the six types of alienation can be best understood by way of syllogism, that is, an argument whereby two opposing ideas are expressed—a thesis and an opposing antithesis— and then a concluding compromise—or synthesis—is finally agreed upon by both debaters. Because the ideological framework of PII involves understanding socioeconomic dynamics beyond oversimplified, often false dichotomies, it embraces a truly innovative solution-driven attitude rooted in dialectical thinking that refuses to throw out the proverbial baby with the bathwater and attempts to devise pragmatic, palatable solutions to people from all ways of thinking and walks of life.

The Six Alienations & Six Movements Towards Reintegration			
ALIENATION FROM:	**DICHOTOMY (THESIS/ANTITHESIS)**	**DIALECTIC (SYNTHESIS)**	**REINTEGRATION MOVEMENT**
ACTIVITY OF LABOR*	OWNER VS WORKER	BUSINESS PARTNERSHIP	ENTREPRENEURIAL
PRODUCT OF LABOR*	INVENTOR VS ASSEMBLER	INDEPENDENT ARTISAN	ARTISANAL
ONE'S OWN SELF*	COMMODITY VS NECESSITY	RECIPROCITY	HOLISTIC HEALTH
OTHER WORKERS*	SUPERIOR VS SUBORDINATE	WORKER-OWNER	CO-OP BUSINESS
COMMUNITY**	SOCIETY VS SELF/FAMILY	SOCIAL NETWORKS	SOCIAL JUSTICE
NATURE**	PROFIT VS PLANET	GREEN BUSINESS	ENVIRONMENTAL

*Marx **ABCrane

Karl Marx—living, theorizing, and writing at a time situated smack dab in the middle of the first and second industrial revolutions—was deeply concerned with the effect that major shifts in industrial production processes and commercialization exerted upon the common laborers. His theory on alienation, perhaps, is most greatly relevant to the fundamental foundation of the overall PII vision and mission that intends to solve for this alienation with an innovative reintegration approach.

Marx saw the origins of the four alienations happening when people moved away from localized, "do-it-yourself-and-for-yourself" simple economies based in small family farming and independent artisanal production processes—and onto the monotonous assembly lines of big business.

The first type that he identifies is the *alienation from one's activity of labor*. When a man or woman builds a home, grows crops, or manufactures shoes for his or her family or immediate community members, they not only experience the gratitude and immediate benefits of the fruits of their labor, but indulge in the pride and skill-building development inherent in the experience of engaging fully in seeing a product grow from seed to root to flower. The magic of this experience, however, gets completely obliterated on the factory assembly line whereby individual workers stand in one lonely, dreary spot all day long performing one repetitive boring task. In the service sector, this type of alienation manifests, too, in a contrived "customer service" persona mask one must wear to please her profit-driven supervisor, manager, and owner of the business for which she works.

With this first type of alienation comes the second—*alienation from the very product of one's labor* efforts. When one engages in producing products and providing services for their family or intimate village community members, those products are directly enjoyed and utilized by their loved ones. There is little difference between the instinctual pride felt by a lioness feeding her cub and a subsistence farmer serving her family a Sunday brunch harvested by her very own hands. But a man slaving on an assembly line producing products for the privileged middle class of a foreign country and securing the profits for a wealthy business owner for whom he works feels the meaningless of his labor; suffers a lack of essential personal purpose of the product itself; and knows that he has been robbed not only of the surplus profit of his hard work, but of the enlivening experience of creative innovation and skill building opportunity enjoyed by the master craftsmen of olden times. Marx referred to this innovation and diverse skill building experience as one's "species essence." Loss of this nature given right of passage—his third type of alienation—was the *alienation of the sense of self*, itself. Finally, the *alienation from other workers* occurs as a result of the first three types of alienations. The isolating assembly line limits time spent meaningfully and playfully with others throughout the workday; limits physical mobility throughout the workplace; often results in the objectification of the worker by customers who see them not as integrated members of the local, intimate community, but as mere functionaries of big corporations driven by profit alone; and spurs contentious competition between employees (e.g., wages, promotions, favoritism, nepotism) that pit exploited laborers against one another.

PII identifies two more types of alienation. The *alienation from community* and *the greater natural environment* have become horrendous over the past century as gluttonous consumer culture has replaced more humble traditional ones rooted in frugal living and a slower-paced lifestyle in general. Keeping-up-with-the-Jones attitudes and shop-'til-you'drop activity has not only subjected the natural environment to devastating exploitation but has destroyed intimate community bonds that are vital to creating and maintaining safe, nurturing spaces for family, friends, and neighbors throughout the world's urban, suburban, and rural spaces.

While it may be more comfortable to think of the alienation human beings experience in their daily work and personal lives as the direct birth-child of one specific economic model or industrial revolution, alienation in its many forms has existed in all modes of economic survival throughout the ages. Hunting and gathering societies seem to exhibit the very opposite of Marxian alienation. Groups of women and men in animal-like packs and herds gathering essentials for their very own purposes coupled with reciprocity between clans, is perhaps the most integrated that members of the human species have ever been. But even these tribes warred with each other—often kidnapping females from each other's tribes to take as their own wives. Subsistence farming communities also enjoyed a great degree of community integration and direct independent resource acquisition and exchange, but perhaps here lies the burgeoning of the great separations to come. The extended and eventually the nuclear family would soon come to alienate the larger tribe with this more sedentary modus operandi of existence. And could not the local village store have been the very advent of the larger multinational conglomerations dominating the market in the 21st century? Feudalism, too, with its strict socioeconomic hierarchies existing within the trade guilds that were very selective and difficult to break into most certainly bred a horrifying sense of alienation within the hearts and minds of peasants suffering the surplus-theft of their labor by the greedy lords of the manor. And the greatest, most tragic irony lies in the so-called Communist countries such as China that have turned out to be the very worst culprits of assembly line horror. (For further explication on the comparison between the four economic models, refer to the essay titled, "The Four Economic Models and The 5th Way Economy," in the author's work *What is Wealth: Thinking Back and Moving Forward* (page 7).

PII's aforementioned attempt to bridge, organize, and unify six present day movements intends to alleviate these six corresponding alienations begins with a transcendence of the dichotomous thinking that tends to dominate the status quo mindset in the 21st century. PII moves beyond this dichotomous thinking towards revealing how allegedly opposing extremes can be harmoniously transformed into complimentary components.

The *entrepreneurial movement*, and more specifically, the *worker-owned cooperative business movement*, are growing at a healthy rate as workers find themselves fed up not only with work place exploitation, but too, the labor union movement that provides little or only superficial relief from the alienation plaguing them. The be-your-own-boss and worker-owned cooperative business models that are cropping up across the globe are perhaps the most profoundly authentic effort to combat the *alienation from one's labor* and *alienation from other laborers*. The false dichotomy between workers and owners, here, resolves itself in the dialectic of the worker-owner model whereby all members of a for-profit business divvy up the workload and profits as earned from their collective efforts.

The alienation from *the product of one's labor* is also being challenged in a significant way. A visit to popular websites such as etsy.com reveals the passionate revival of the *artisanal* mode of production long forgotten in the hustle and bustle of the sweat shop and shopping malls that have come to dominate production models in the last couple of centuries. The Etsy business model provides a viable marketplace for the DIY artist and artisanal community to advertise and retail products that they themselves innovate, design, build, assemble, and deliver single handedly or in intimate business partnerships with friends and near-by associates. While workers holding jobs in the mainstream marketplace must find a fulfilling outlet for the expression of their species essence in various hobbies during limited leisure time, the new artisans of today are churning enough profits to be able to quit their day jobs and basque in the glow of their authentic selves every day—and on their own time.

"Just as in religion the spontaneous activity of the human imagination, of the human brain and the human heart, operates independently of the individual—that is, operates on him as an alien, divine or diabolical activity—so is the worker's activity not his spontaneous activity. It belongs to another; it is the loss of his self." (Marx, *Economic and Philosophic Manuscripts of 1844*). Here, Marx speaks of yet another tragic consequence of working menial jobs in the sweat shops and storefronts. When one's source of authority has been externalized from his self—whether as a God or employer—he inevitably begins to experience what Marx referred to as *alienation from self*. As mass migrations of people have turned both the USA and the entire globe into the proverbial melting pot, many Eastern cultural, spiritual, and philosophical practices have caught the deep interest of many westerners. Feeling so deeply alienated by the modern materialistic way of life, it is no wonder that the *Holistic Health Movement* so chockfull of yoga, tai chi, herbal medicine, acupuncture, and so many body-mind-spirit healing activities have gained such popularity. It seems, then, that the *alienation from self* experienced in today's world is somewhat remedied by these practices that once again ground people in their bodies and nourish them with the deep sense of purpose and connection to the communities that have cropped up around such activities. In one arm is the brief case, while tucked under the other, a yoga mat that promises to alleviate all the stress and alienation experienced in the typical 9 to 5 work day of the common worker.

In alignment with the Holistic Health Movement are the *Social Justice and Environmental Movements* rapidly spreading across the world to combat the tragic consequences that have ensued due to our *alienation from community and nature*. Fed up with the complacency and cruelty of indifferent governments, citizens across the world have taken to the streets in protest; started nonprofits that help to tackle a variety of human rights and environmental issues; and have launched green businesses that bring healthy, organic, and sustainable products to local and global market zones.

Project Integrity International bridges these six critical—yet often scattered, redundant, and disorganized—movements with the afore-discussed cooperative franchise model that will serve to solve for these inefficiencies within and in between the various movements. By keeping a bright constantly strobing light upon the alienation that has been plaguing humankind for centuries, PII brings about a new paradigm that will not only alleviate the current alienation facing humankind, but prevent its re-manifestation for future generations.

THE UNIVERSAL CONDITION OF HUMANKIND

In today's world, we are unfortunately witnessing epidemic levels of deprivation of our needs in our communities and nations. Human ignorance, greed, and corruption are the root causes of the wide-scale deprivation and economic failure facing humankind. More than a business and economic system, Project Integrity International is an international community that takes a proactive approach to addressing human issues.

SIX UNIVERSAL CONCERNS & EPIDEMICS OF HUMANKIND

The Universal Condition of Humankind	
Six Universal Concerns	**Six Universal Epidemics**
Air & Nutrition	Pollution & Famine
Sexuality & Reproduction	Rape & Eugenics
Housing & Transportation	Homelessness & Overcrowding
Community & Communication	War & Disorder
Education & Enlightenment	Ignorance & Corruption
Healing & Spirituality	Disease & Depression

Air & Nutrition; Pollution & Famine

Throughout history, human beings have struggled against forces of nature, such as droughts, floods, storms, and forest fires that have diminished their available local and global food supply. Today, we are experiencing epidemic levels of air pollution, obesity, famine, and food contamination that appeared when the greed of agribusiness began to feed consumer addiction while ignoring basic human needs. When we neglect to address the first universal concern, Air and Nutrition, individuals and societies can literally die within just moments or days. PII's nutritionists, agriculturalists, air quality specialists, and franchisees will help to restore abundance, health, and balance to the local and global food supply.

Sexuality & Reproduction; Rape & Eugenics

Statistics reveal alarmingly high rates of rape, child sexual abuse, sex slavery, unwanted pregnancies, sexual dysfunction, sexually transmitted diseases, and other expressions of our sexual ignorance in all countries of the world. Eugenics—the social philosophy that advocates the improvement of human hereditary traits through various forms of intervention—has also posed a horrendous problem when used to justify forced human sterilization and genocide. When we neglect to address the second universal concern, Sexuality and Reproduction, human beings suffer sexual dysfunction, population imbalances, and act out with sexual violence. PII's sexual health professionals will modernize and enlighten sexual education; challenge the exploitive aspects of the sexual entertainment industry; work to eradicate black market sex slavery; and restore health to human sexual expression and reproduction. Critically, by creating alternative economic opportunities, PII will provide a viable refuge for women and children who are made vulnerable to sex slavery by their life circumstances.

Housing & Transportation; Homelessness & Overcrowding

With a significant increase in natural disasters across the globe in recent decades, implementing more environmentally efficient technologies and innovations must become a priority for the human race. When we neglect to address the third universal concern, Housing and Transportation, human species perish without protection from temperature extremes, natural disasters, ineffective mobility, and technological accidents. Community restructuring efforts must tackle the problems of widespread homelessness, slums, and overcrowding that affect every neighborhood, city, and country across the world. By designing, producing, and providing durable and sustainable housing, transportation systems, and other technologies, PII helps to more effectively shelter and transport the world's population.

Community and Communications; War & Disorder

Corporate, government, and nonprofit bureaucracies across the globe are plagued with greed, corruption, fraud, inefficiency, and other internal abuses that contribute to the world epidemics of social disorder and war. When we neglect to address the fourth universal concern, Community and Communication, human beings becomes socially dysfunctional en masse, turning nations into war zones. PII fosters healthy interpersonal relations and provides sustainable communication technologies that benefit individuals, businesses, organizations, and communities.

Education & Enlightenment; Ignorance & Corruption

A myriad of ills within both the public and private educational systems across the globe impedes the physical, intellectual, and spiritual growth of the world's youth. When we neglect to address the fifth universal concern, Education and Enlightenment, human beings become helpless in all matters of both physical survival and spiritual fulfillment. PII provides educational methods, tools, and facilities that combat intellectual ignorance and moral corruption by fostering the healthy functioning of mind, body, and spirit alike while preparing individuals for future success in all areas of life.

Healing & Spirituality; Disease & Depression

Today's world is witnessing alarming levels of physical disease and emotional depression. When we neglect to address the sixth universal concern, Spirituality and Healing, human beings become physically, emotionally, and mentally diseased. PII provides safe, affordable, and effective medicines and healing procedures to people across all nations.

When the six universal concerns are not met—or are met inefficiently—individuals and communities begin to deteriorate. A vicious cycle, the six epidemics cause and perpetuate one another. Lack of adequate nutrition, for example, leads to all kinds of physical and mental illness, while poorly designed housing and transportation systems pollute our skies, water, and land.

Conversely, addressing one universal concern means addressing all of them. Ensuring greater reproductive rights and economic opportunities for women improves the circumstances of the entire community in which they live. School breakfast programs have proven to significantly improve students' educational achievement. Green technologies not only lesson the pressure on sensitive habitats but increase spiritual connectedness to the natural environment. PII's WISR Franchises directly remedy the epidemics by providing healthy goods, services, employment, education, and entertainment venues that restore health and balance to individuals, communities, and the greater natural environment.

THE UNIVERSAL STRUCTURE OF THE NATION-STATE

In a world so full of violence, disease, depression, war, and environmental pollution, one must ask: Why? In examining the structure and inner workings both within and between nation-states, we can gain better insight. Much of human suffering is avoidable, unnecessary, and even consciously created. Most modern nations have wide gaps between their rich and poor—and those gaps are glued in place by our irrational and destructive lust for power over others. All nation-states are characterized by a universal power structure that exists not only between the rich and the poor, but within each of the entities of which all nation-states are comprised.

THE EIGHT ENTITIES OF THE NATION-STATE

PII posits a model of the modern nation-state consisting of eight constituent entities—namely, corporate consumerism (including media), nuclear family, organized religion, public education, work force, police force, military force, and political force. These entities each play a distinct role in producing and maintaining the nation-state of which they are a part. On a physical-economic dimension, the entities of our world's nation-states function to feed, clothe, house, transport, educate, protect, and entertain us. On a spiritual-political dimension, the nation-state serves to provide its citizens with a sense of unity, order, and "patriotic morale" necessary to motivate citizens to work together to keep the system functioning.

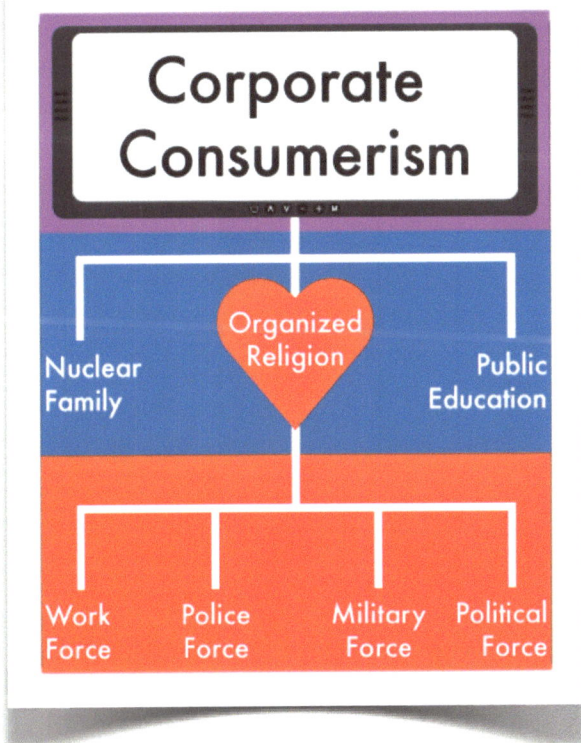

The first entity—consumerism—is the goal entity. Put simply, consumerism is the individual and collective utilization of goods and services. It involves such activities as eating food, fueling cars, watering gardens, and purchasing products. Consumerism is the result of our drives to meet our needs and satisfy our desires, whether as individuals, communities, or nations. In the twentieth century, the entertainment industry and media came to dominate our consumer-driven lifestyles and purchasing habits. Therefore, it is critical to understand how these two sub-entities also affect our consciousness and behavior.

The next three entities—nuclear family, organized religion, and public education—mold the youth of the nation into future adults who will become the actors in the work force, police force, military force, and political force. In their formative years, children formulate ideas, attitudes, and actions about their world from their families, religious authorities, and educators. These entities prepare the youth for their future roles as workers, consumers, soldiers, and voters.

The Human Hierarchy

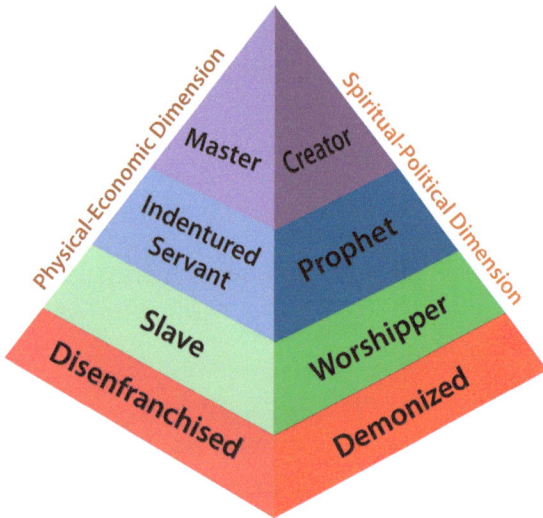

THE HUMAN HIERARCHY

Each entity seems to share in common a four-layered hierarchy, or chain of command. Furthermore, real experience and scientific studies reveal similar corruption and abuse patterns occurring within each entity. At the highest layer of the hierarchy are the Master-Creators, or the "top dogs," controlling the layers below. On the physical-economic dimension, the Master determines the flow of goods, services, and capital within a family, community, or nation. On the spiritual-political dimension, the Creator sets moral codes, writes the laws, and dictates status quo cultural practices. At the middle layer of the hierarchy are the Indentured Servant-Prophets, or the middle men, controlling the layers below but controlled by the layers above. On the physical-economic dimension, the Indentured Servant serves as a buffer zone between the highest and lowest layers by managing the flow of goods and services within a family, community, or nation. On the spiritual-political dimension, the Prophet teaches, preaches, and proselytizes the commands of the Creator to the bottom-most layers. At the lowest layer of the hierarchy are the Slave-Worshippers, or "bottom dogs," controlled by all of the layers above. On the physical-economic dimension, the Slave toils to satisfy the physical needs and desires of the levels above. On the spiritual-political dimension, the Worshipper obeys and follows the moral codes, laws, and cultural practices determined by the upper levels. Finally, at the very bottom, are the disenfranchised and demonized—the dropouts, convicts, runaways, refugees, homeless, illegal immigrants, and others banned from the rights and privileges granted to the greater society.

Many problems of epidemic magnitude arise from the structure of these hierarchies. Consumerism degrades both the environment and consumers with its lure of endless toxic treats. Master-level business owners profit from goods and services, Indentured Servant-level marketers and advertisers use communications media to manipulate Slave-level customers to buy those goods and services. Without marketers and advertisers, owners would not be able to sell enough products to make a profit. By manipulating human instinct, intellectual ignorance, and emotional vulnerability, advertisers seduce customers into buying unnecessary goods that often degrade labor, customers, and the greater natural environment.

THE UNIVERSAL STRUCTURE OF THE NATION-STATE

DIMENSION ROLE	HEAVEN	PURGATORY	EARTH	HELL
PHYSICAL-ECONOMIC ROLE	MASTER	INDENTURED SERVANT	SLAVE	DISENFRANCHISED (PASSIVE/ACTIVE)
SPIRITUAL-POLITICAL ACTOR	CREATOR	PROPHET	WORSHIPPER	DEMONIZED
CORPORATE CONSUMERISM	OWNER	MARKETER	CUSTOMER	BANKRUPT/ BOYCOTT
NUCLEAR FAMILY	FATHER	MOTHER	CHILD	ORPHANED/ RUN-AWAY
ORGANIZED RELIGION	POPE-FIGURE	CLERGY	WORSHIPPER	EX-COMMUNICATED/ AGNOSTIC
PUBLIC EDUCATION	PRINCIPAL	TEACHER	STUDENT	EXPELLED/ DROP-OUT
WORK FORCE	OWNER	MANAGER	WORKER	UNEMPLOYED/ SELF-EMPLOYED
POLICE FORCE	CHIEF	POLICE/GUARD	CONVICT	PAROLEE/ ESCAPEE
MILITARY FORCE	PRESIDENT	GENERAL	TROOPER	DISCHARGED/ CONSCIENTIOUS OBJECTOR
POLITICAL FORCE	POLITICIAN	LOBBYIST	VOTER	JIM CROWED/ IGNORANT

In the nuclear family, Master-level fathers have traditionally held the position of "head of household," making major decisions, dishing out punishment, and controlling the finances. Indentured Servant-level mothers, traditionally the primary caregivers, take commands from above and deliver them below to Slave-level children. Despite the recent challenging of harsh and punitive child-rearing techniques, incidents of child abuse and spouse battery presently occur in alarming proportions across all classes, races, and nations.

Within organized religion, we have the latest scandal of sexual abuse of children by Indentured Servant-level priests—who are protected by Master-level popes and bishops who consciously enable them to continue the abuse. Slave-level worshippers at the bottom often look the other way in obedience to religious authorities and in compliance with societal norms.

Within the public educational system, we have many wonderful, kind teachers, but we also have the power-hungry Indentured Servant-level teachers who humiliate, bore, and otherwise abuse their Slave-level students with threats of being sent to the Master-level principal's office. All too often, children are harshly told what to think and how to be rather than encouraged to critically think for themselves. Further, only in the twentieth century has the use of physical punishment by teachers against students begun to be challenged and legally banned.

Within the work force, there are all kinds of labor abuses, such as underpay, overwork, toxic work environments, and sexual harassment. With the Master-level owners making most of the profits and the Slave-level laborers doing most of the work for little pay, these kinds of abuses are inevitable. Indentured Servant-level managers and supervisors take orders and accept rewards from above for controlling the levels below.

Within the police force and military force, there are guards who abuse prisoners, officers who batter innocent suspects, and military commanders who rape subordinates and foreign civilians. As in organized religion, Master-level captains, sergeants, and other high-ranking officials pass orders down the chain of command. Indentured Servant-level police, prison guards, and soldiers do the life-endangering dirty work of arresting, detaining, capturing, and killing of lower Slave-level criminal suspects, national scapegoats, and war enemies. Tragically, many such suspects are falsely accused, unjustly punished, racially profiled, or outright framed.

In politics we witness embarrassing levels of bribery, embezzlement, election fraud, and greed-driven lobbyist pandering. Master-level politicians write laws and regulations that benefit Indentured Servant-level corporate and "special interest" lobbyists, yet hinder Slave-level voters at the bottom.

The three-leveled hierarchies comprising the nation-state are not always corrupt or destructive. Many well-meaning individuals are to be found in all entities and levels. Corruption and destructive behaviors are exhibited at all levels as well. However, the very structure is inherently damaging in that it divides and conquers individuals into political, economic, and cultural roles that limit growth, variety, and security of both the individual and the collective. While the lower levels are barred from essential decision-making processes that intimately affect their lives, the pencil-pushing upper levels are barred from engagement in the hard work that strengthens body and exercises direct survival skills. The laborers at the bottom find themselves bored by the repetitive and meaningless nature of their "work," while the owners at the top often feel the hollowness of a lifestyle that revolves around endless materialistic pursuit. As statistics reveal, depression, disease, substance abuse, familial dysfunction, and other hardships are being experienced at all levels of society in epidemic proportions.

Although all living species exhibit natural hierarchical behavior, the human hierarchies that dominate modern nation-states have become distorted and exaggerated in a way that creates havoc within human communities, nations, and the natural environment. A peculiarity of human hierarchies is that unwritten and written moral codes often "teach" individuals at all levels their "duty" to blindly obey their masters, bosses, parents, politicians, and religious leaders. Unlike wild animals, religious and political leaders use the preconceived threat of punishment and the promise of rewards to keep people firmly in their places. While wild animals fight or play dead to avoid their enemies' advances, lower-level humans often passively accept punishment from their superiors—believing that they somehow "deserve it."

Thus, although hierarchical behavior and dominance are perhaps hard-wired into our genes, their modern expression are detrimentally contrived, exaggerated, and distorted in the mirror of our ideas. So if it is our negative and limiting ideas about ourselves that cause us so much suffering, it stands to reason that positive and unlimited ideas about ourselves have the power to alleviate our suffering. PII offers an out from this dead-end of societal dysfunction by embracing and realizing a more enlightened vision of the human species' unlimited potential.

PROJECT INTEGRITY INTERNATIONAL: A NEW MODEL FOR HUMANITY

Although the three-leveled hierarchies greatly dominate our families, communities, organizations, and nations, many alternative structures that promote mutual respect, equality, and group cooperation exist in great numbers throughout the world. These structures include various indigenous tribes, youth communes, co-ops, workers' unions, women's empowerment groups, spiritual circles, and other organizations that emphasize democratic decision-making and group collaboration. Furthermore, many members of three-leveled hierarchies choose to interact with each other in a respectful, democratic manner. Policies on sexual harassment, fair compensation, worker safety, child labor laws, and a myriad of other laws are designed to protect all levels of the hierarchies, whether at school, work, home, or anywhere else.

As an international franchise of ecosustainable co-ops, Project Integrity International provides a healthier, egalitarian structure for individuals who wish to escape the destructive and limiting hierarchies that dominate their lives. Project Integrity International promotes equality and balance not only between humans but also within the natural environment.

THE ECONOMICS OF PROJECT INTEGRITY INTERNATIONAL

THE PRODUCE-DISTRIBUTE-CONSUME-DISPOSE CYCLE

An "economic system" is a structure by which a community, organization, nation, or world produces, distributes, consumes, and disposes of goods and services. All regional, national, and global economic systems across the world, in one or another manner, consist of this cycle.

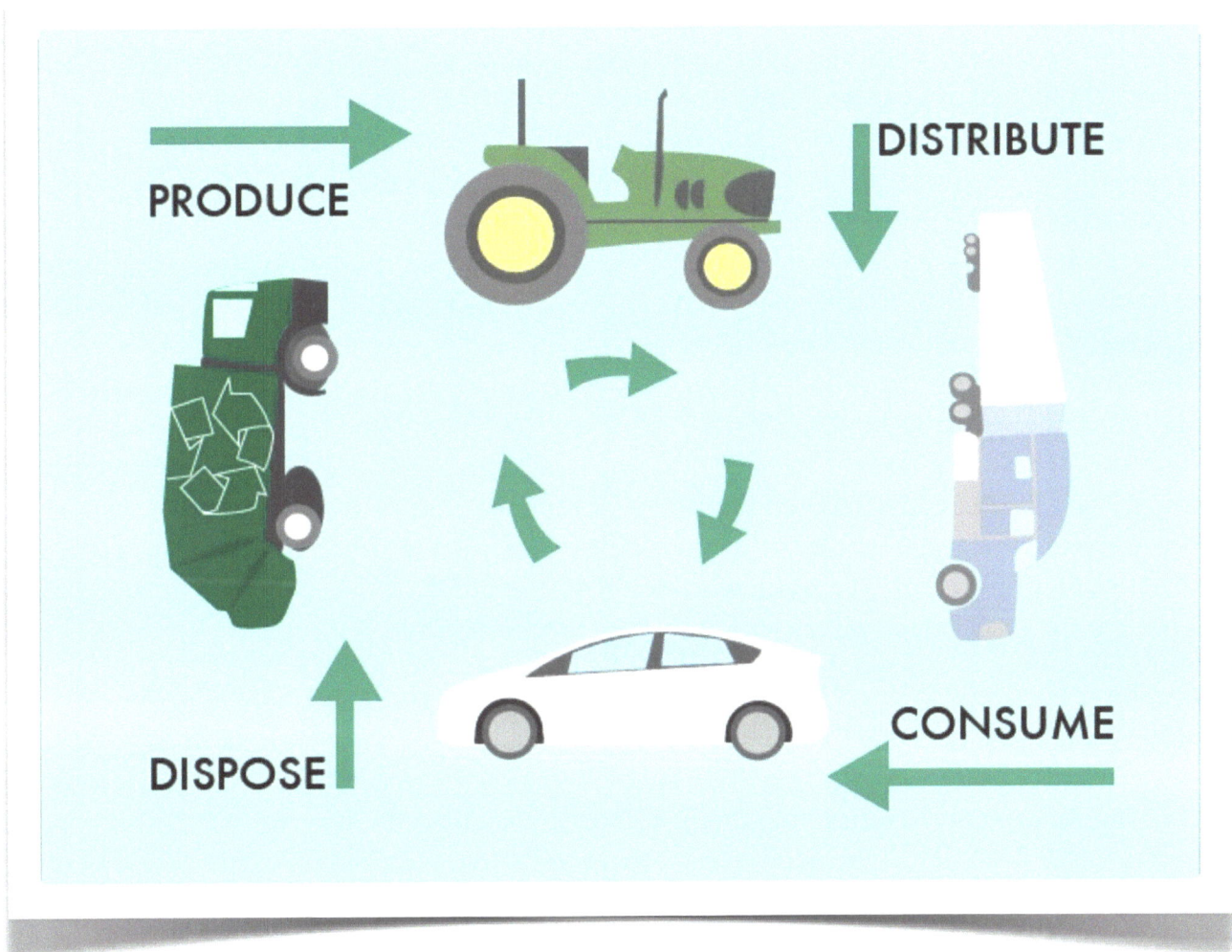

The production of goods and services encompasses the innovation and invention of new concepts and technologies, the extraction of raw resources, the processing and packaging of products, and the planning of business operations. Production takes place on the land where resources are extracted; in the laboratory where they are tested, altered, and refined; in the factory where they are assembled and packaged; and in storage facilities and business offices where they are prepared for sale in the marketplace. Producers include farmers, crop pickers, factory workers, inventors, industrial designers, laboratory scientists, businesspersons, and others who prepare goods and services for sale in the marketplace.

Distribution takes place when goods and services are moved from their place of production to warehouses and storefronts where they are sold in wholesale and retail markets. Airplanes, ships, trains, trucks, vans, bicycles, and foot-carriers deliver resources and products across cities, countries, and the globe to be bought and consumed by the worlds' customers. With the popularization of internet shopping, computers, too, are active vehicles for the transportation of ideas, financial transactions, and other forms of communication. Distributors include truck drivers, dock workers, ship and airplane crews, and internet shopping site personnel.

Consumption happens when goods and services are sold, bought, and used by wholesalers, retailers, and clients. Customers and clients purchase goods and services from warehouses, stores, malls, farmer's markets, on the internet, and from other market fronts. These products include both our basic necessities and our most desired luxuries. All human beings across the globe consume goods and services, poor and rich alike.

Finally, the disposal of goods happens when unused, wasted materials are brought to dumps, landfills, or recycling facilities. Dumps, landfills, and recycling plants store, process, and otherwise manage waste products, such as discarded packaging, broken or unwanted technology, and other such "leftovers." Persons involved in waste management include municipally employed garbage collectors, consumers who collect and sell back recyclable materials, junk yard dealers, recycled material retailers, and both municipal and private-sector recycling plant workers.

The significance of understanding the economic cycle of Produce-Distribute-Consume-Dispose lies in gaining better insight into the strengths and weaknesses of the greater economy. An examination of our world reveals tragic rates of pollution, corruption, unnecessary waste, diseases, and other atrocities that can be traced in great part to the inefficiency and abuses of our local and global economic systems. Only when we closely examine the flow of goods and services between producers, distributors, and consumers can we begin to pinpoint problems and devise solutions.

THE TWELVE ESSENTIAL ELEMENTS OF EFFECTIVE ECONOMY

The effective functioning of the Produce-Distribute-Consume-Dispose Cycles operating across the globe depends on the adequate presence of twelve essential elements. These parts of the greater economy are necessary to keep people fed, clothed, transported, housed, educated, and entertained.

The twelve elements are made up of six pairs of "complementary components." That is, each pair represents two elements that are exchanged for and balanced against each other. For example, "incentives" and "labor" are exchanged within the greater economy. Workers trade their labor for incentives or pay. Incentives can take the form of monetary payments, profits, vacation time, or health-care benefits. Without incentives and without laborers who work for them, businesses and economic systems would not be able to function. To understand how the twelve essential elements operate separately and together is a critical first step in improving our individual and collective economic lives.

The first pair of essential economic elements are vision and discipline. All business concepts and inventions begin with a "vision"—that is, they are conjured up in the mind as an idea before they are realized in concrete reality as a product or service. All products and services in the marketplace emerge from someone's imagination, and only later manifest as something tangible. Together, the effort, drive, and endurance necessary to bring visions into fruition is called "discipline." Without discipline, visions would remain mere figments of our imagination. A successful business or economic system balances vision with discipline by matching great ideas with hard work. As products and services are being diligently produced, the inner visionary remains awake to possibilities for continual improvements.

The second pair of essential economic elements are energy and resources. All products and services in the marketplace are comprised of energy and raw materials. Energy is the fuel that is necessary to extract resources, refine products, and distribute goods and services. Resources are the natural and manufactured ingredients that comprise a given product or service. Efficient production of products and services depends on the adequate presence of energy and resources. The conversion processes of energy into resources, and of resources back into energy, must maximize efficiency and minimize waste in order for factories, laboratories, businesses, and storefronts to function properly.

The third pair of essential economic elements are knowledge and know-how. Possessing many kinds of expertise is critical to the functional production, distribution, and consumption of all goods and services. Experts in bringing products to the marketplace include scientists, financial advisors, technical specialists, marketers, artists, and business administrators. Once gathered, knowledge and information are converted into producing, distributing, and consuming products and services. Know-how is just that—knowing how to do something. Doctors prescribe medicines, but nurses administer them. Scientists, engineers, and architects invent machines and design homes, but technicians and construction workers build and repair them. Knowledge and know-how, necessary complements of the same functional whole, must be continually updated and implemented to keep pace with a rapidly changing global economic and technological climate.

The fourth pair of essential economic elements are incentives and labor. Incentives, or pay, are all the rewards, such as profits, compensation, health care benefits, and vacation time, for which laborers and businesspersons exchange their work. The effective operation of a business or economic system must attract enough laborers to produce, distribute, and sell its products and services. Without proper incentives, workers will either refuse to work, go on strike for better pay and hours, or simply slack off on the job. Therefore, a business or economic system must profit enough to hire and maintain an effective labor base to carry out its tasks.

The fifth pair of essential economic elements are time and space. In the economic sense, time is the amount of hours, days, months, and years necessary to produce, distribute, and consume products and services. Critical to the effective functioning of businesses and economic systems across the globe, time must be measured, planned, and conserved. A wasted moment can cause a ship to sink, a deal to fall through, or a delivery truck to slip off the edge of a road. Time can be the amount of minutes to produce one unit of product, the amount of days to ship a product, or the amount of years for a business to open up additional branches. Space, or real estate, is the land, buildings, roadways, and storefronts that are utilized to bring goods and services into fruition. It is essential that time and space are balanced in a way that benefits producers, distributors, and consumers.

The sixth pair of essential economic elements are capital and clientele. Here, capital represents both the monetary and technological reserves of a given business or economic system. It includes the wholesale and retail products for sale in the marketplace, the technology and land involved in their production, and the monetary profits gained from their sale. A business' or economic system's clientele are all the consumers who buy its products or services. For proper functioning, a business or economic system must not only generate enough products or services, but attract enough clients and customers to purchase them. Therefore, levels of available capital and clientele must be carefully monitored and balanced to avoid obstacles and keep the economy prospering.

The twelve essential elements must be individually refined and collectively harmonized to maintain and enhance the economic situation for all participants. Many problems in our current global economic systems can be traced to either qualitative or quantitative inadequacies of one or more of the twelve essentials of effective economy. As a parallel economic system, PII will strive to continually fine-tune and organize these twelve essentials in order to create a better economy for everyone.

THE FOUR ROLE-PLAYERS OF ECONOMY

All businesses and economic systems are started, run, and patronized by four main role-players—owners, workers, shareholders, and clients.

Owners are those individuals who possess the deeds to real estate, factories, warehouses, stores, internet shopping sites, and the like. Workers are all those individuals who are employed and compensated by owners, such as supervisors, managers, office assistants, and manual laborers. Clients and customers are the people who purchase products and services from business owners. Finally, shareholders are all those individuals who own shares, or percentages, of a company's capital holdings. Shareholders include silent partners, financial lenders, and anyone who has purchased shares of a company on the stock market.

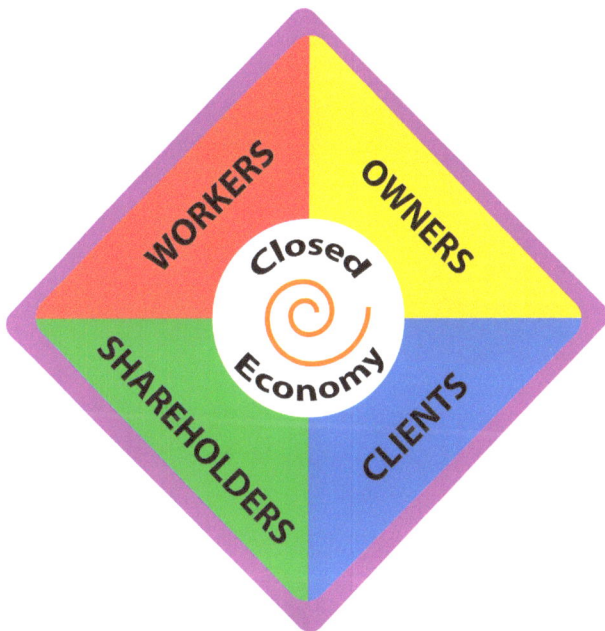

Many problems exist among the four role-players within businesses and the greater economy, such as financial scandals, employee abuses, consumer manipulation, infighting, miscommunication, and gross imbalances of wealth. Throughout history, dysfunction and imbalances between these role-players of economy have plagued the human species. With the growth of industry and the spread of rampant consumerism across continents and countries, the inequalities among the four role-players have increased at alarming rates. This growth and expansion of the economy has widened the distance between owners, workers, shareholders, and clients as factories have moved abroad to countries that supply cheap labor, as the internet has allowed customers to buy products from afar, and as shareholders have begun to buy up shares of companies with which they have no other affiliation. As larger businesses and corporations have begun to replace small family businesses, the relationships among owners, workers, shareholders, and clients have grown more physically and emotionally distant—leaving more room for waste and corruption to leak in. No longer do owners, workers, shareholders, and clients live in the same town, community, or even country. No longer do they stand face to face in everyday business dealings. Thus, no longer do they stand on common ground, form intimate community bonds, or connect on similar values. Less direct control over our short-term and long-term economic fate has inevitably led to the cruel realities of waste and corruption. By closing the gap between owners, workers, shareholders, and clients, PII alleviates this alienation and improves economic circumstances for all.

THE WASTE-CORRUPTION POTENTIAL

The Waste-Corruption Potential increases as the distance increases between a product's place of production and its place of consumption; and as workers, owners, shareholders, and clients grow more alienated from each other. While it takes negligible amounts of time, space, energy, knowledge, and capital to transfer homegrown vegetables from one's backyard to one's kitchen, it takes a great quantity of these to deliver sufficient volumes of vegetables between states, countries, and continents. Because more individuals, organizations, governments, and facilities are involved in the latter case, the potential for human corruption, error, and folly increase as well.

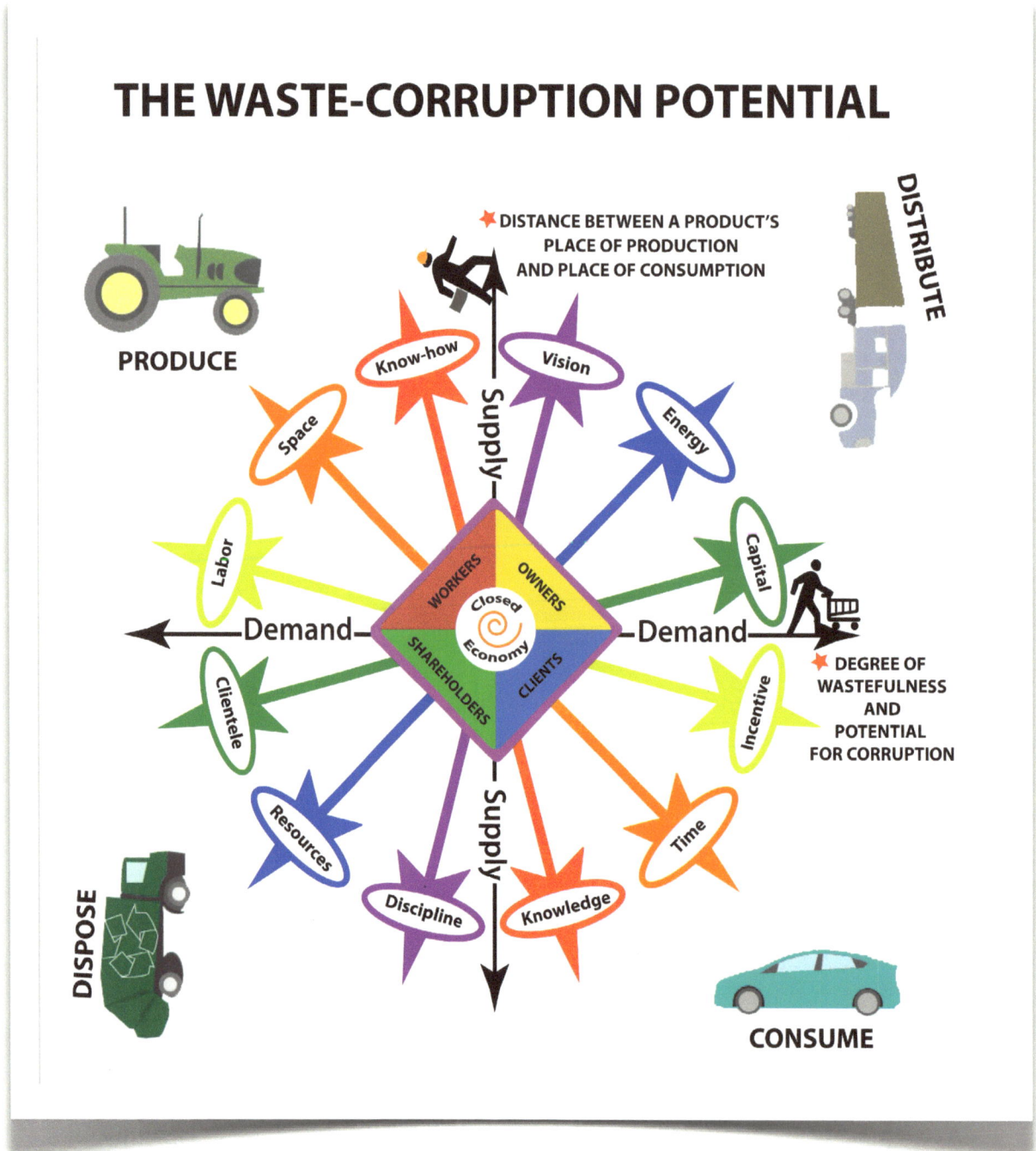

THE WASTE-CORRUPTION POTENTIAL

★ DISTANCE BETWEEN A PRODUCT'S PLACE OF PRODUCTION AND PLACE OF CONSUMPTION

DISTRIBUTE

PRODUCE

Know-how   Vision   Energy

Space   Capital

Labor

Demand   WORKERS   OWNERS   Demand
Closed Economy
SHAREHOLDERS   CLIENTS

★ DEGREE OF WASTEFULNESS AND POTENTIAL FOR CORRUPTION

Clientele   Incentive

Resources   Time

Discipline   Knowledge

DISPOSE

CONSUME

To be aware of the Waste-Corruption Potential as it plays out in our current local and global economies is the first step in reducing waste, corruption, and other inefficiencies plaguing our individual and collective existence.

CLOSED ECONOMY

The Waste-Corruption Potential can be reduced by spurring the growth of small businesses and integrated local economic communities. Doing so will inevitably foster communal intimacy, common purpose, and economic equality, and thus yield stronger protection against corruption, waste, and inefficiency.

Many small businesses, co-ops, and local farms today are doing just that! PII will be structured as a closed economy—that is, an economic system in which the four role-players overlap, each one playing every role at once. As an international franchise of sustainable co-ops, PII eliminates the distance between participants. Ideally, a co-op is a business in which all the owners possess equal numbers of shares, and in which all the owners do the same amount and type of work. Because PII encourages its franchisees to purchase products and services from other PII franchise stores, the owners are also the predominant clients and customers. Finally, because all franchisees own equal shares in the larger PII umbrella corporation, all are primary shareholders as well. As a closed economy, PII will reduce the Waste-Corruption Potential by ensuring that all participants receive their fair share and by making locally accessible the twelve essentials of economy. With this newfound economic and emotional security, intimacy, and connectedness, participants will decreasingly be compelled toward corrupt and wasteful behavior.

NEED-DRIVEN ECONOMY VS. ADDICTION-DRIVEN ECONOMY

Although our current global economic system provides for basic needs such as food, clothing, shelter, and transportation, it also manufactures luxuries such as non-educational toys, junk food, and other products and services that are unnecessary—and often harmful—to consumers and the greater natural environment. Furthermore, many of these luxuries are being consumed by economically privileged individuals at the expense of the basic survival needs of less fortunate persons who slave in factories to produce them. Moreover, the labor-intensive production of many of these luxuries is destroying the natural environment at alarming rates; enslaving laborers to long days of repetitive, mind-numbing work with little compensation; and promoting a consumeristic, dog-eat-dog lifestyle devoid of spiritual meaning.

Our current addiction-driven economy has indeed taken over. Subsistence farmers, who traditionally have fed their families and communities with fruits, vegetables, and grains, are being replaced by large agribusiness plantation owners who turn the land into junk food, alcohol, cigarettes, and other "poisons-for-profit." The former indigenous subsistence farmers end up slaving for the very corporations that brutally pushed them off their homelands in the first place! Gas-guzzling vehicles and flimsy, timber-intensive houses pollute the skies and deplete the rain-forests, while public transportation systems deteriorate and sturdier building designs fail to be implemented. Violent video games, dumb-downing toys, and games of domination further encourage a meaningless lifestyle of quick fixes, cheap thrills, gratuitous violence, and rampant consumerism.

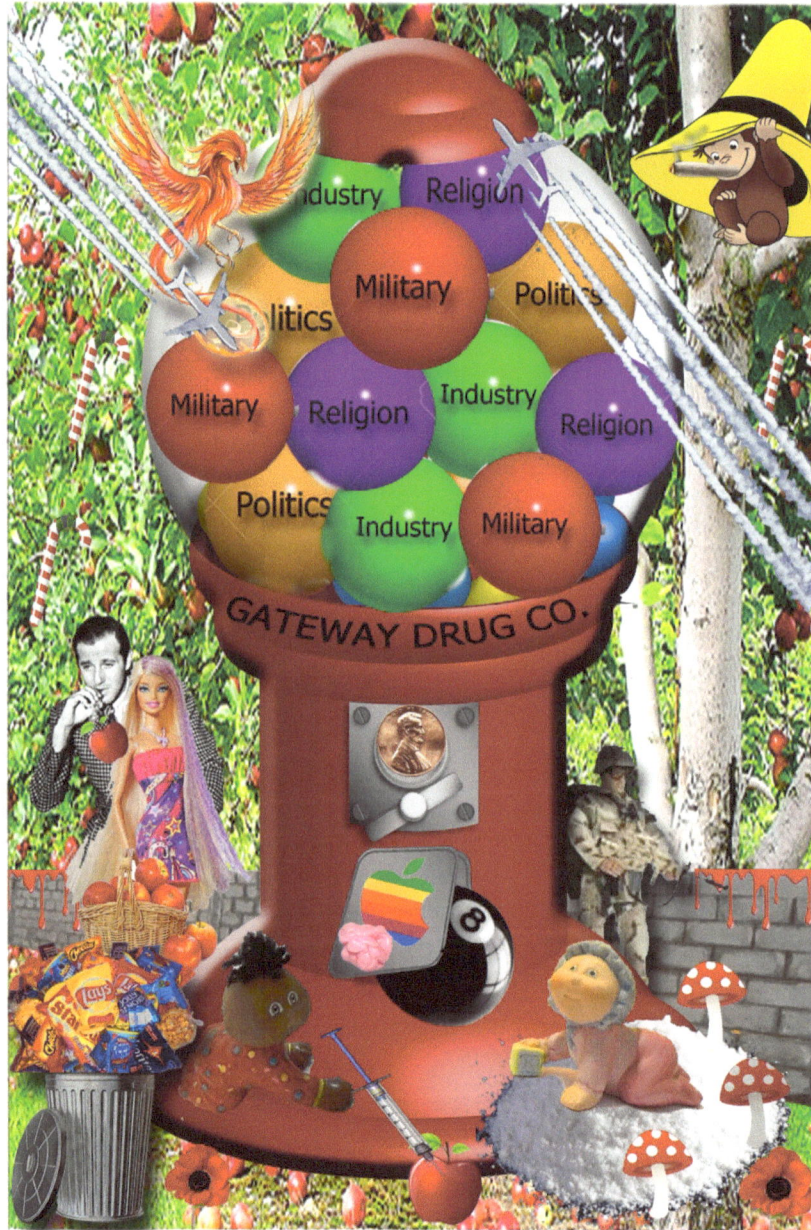

"Gateway Drug" ABCrane 2017

Conversely, PII focuses on providing our most basic needs while eliminating excesses that prove useless and harmful to consumers and the natural environment alike. As a need-driven economy, PII will focus its efforts on providing healthy and ecosustainable food, clothing, transportation, housing, education, and entertainment venues. Doing so will not only provide individuals and communities with what they need, but will eliminate from the marketplace those products and services that are unnecessary and harmful.

As the global economy makes the shift from greed and addiction to need and balance, the natural environment will make the critical shift from depletion to restoration, from illness to health, and from scarcity to abundance.

NEED-BASED ECONOMY VS. WORK-ETHIC-BASED ECONOMY

Most nations of the world are troubled by unemployment and underemployment. Popular media, governments, big business, and mainstream educational establishments tote the idea that the solution to unemployment is to "create more jobs." More often than not, these establishments band together to do just that. Municipal, state, and federal governments often grant tax breaks, subsidies, and other rewards to large corporations and multinationals who open factories and storefronts in areas with low employment rates. Although these "big businesses" reek havoc on communities by driving out mom-and-pops, creating more environmental pollution, and encouraging gross consumerism, the justification for their existence lies in that they "create more jobs." Although this is true, many of these jobs offer meager wages, no benefits, little room for advancement, and a lifetime of drudge work. Nonetheless, people need to eat, and to eat one needs a job.

In more simple economic systems, such as hunting and gathering and subsistence farming, the members of the economic community pitch in to provide for their individual and collective survival necessities. So if there are ten houses to be built, three fields to be plowed, and one hundred animals to be herded in a thousand member community, each person will more or less do a thousandth of the work necessary to ensure that everyone's basic needs get met. With the shift from these simple economies into feudalistic and capitalistic ones that stressed making profits, the commodification of labor, and consumerism as a way of life, a "work ethic" emerged. More than providing basic needs for one's self, family, and intimate community, "work" became increasingly about competing with neighbors, associates, and friends in the game of materialism. Working forty or more hours a week became the status quo standard for everyone, including droves of women across the globe who pried their way into the male-dominated workforce. No longer was work about directly growing, building, and maintaining one's own familial and tribal nest. Instead, the masses in so-called developed and underdeveloped countries alike slaved to turn the planet into one big toxic concrete cage filled with all kinds of needless junk. Work was no longer merely the practical means of survival—it was now a moral ethic that saturated the collective consciousness of the toiling masses. To be a bum, a starving artist, a wondering poet, or a welfare recipient became a thing of shame, while the workaholics and over-achievers were rewarded, honored, and worshipped. Of course, there is certainly nothing wrong with hard work. But our current global "work-ethic-based" economy, in the process of "creating more jobs in the name of economic prosperity," precipitates mass poverty, spreads pollution, encourages destructive consumerism, and diminishes leisure time.

Need-Based Economy VS. "Work-Ethic"- Based Economy

Wr="real" annual work hours per worker
Wa="arbitrary" annual work hours per worker
X=# of workers in given economic zone
Y=# of annual "real" work hours in given economic zone
Z=# of annual "arbitrary" work hours in given economic zone
{ $Z=2080X$ (based on 40-hour work week)
U=unnecessary work hours in given economic zone

Need-Based Economy

$$Wr=Y/X$$

*0% unemployment achieved by elimination of arbitrary work and redistribution of real work yielding greater leisure time per worker

"Work-Ethic"-Based Economy

$$Wa=Z/X$$
$$Wa=(2080X)/X$$
$$Wa=2080$$

*unemployment ensues when $X>Z$

Unnecessary Work Hours in Given Economic Zone
$$U=Wa-Wr$$

If one were to determine the number of hours of work necessary to provide for all the basic needs of any given community, and then subtract that number from the actual number of work that the members are laboring in order to produce a plethora of toxic and unnecessary goods and services, one will be shocked by the amount of time, resources, energy, and land wasted by their participation in the work-ethic-based economy.

PII, as a need-based economy, will eliminate that grave waste by localizing economies, reducing distribution expenditures, discouraging a consumeristic lifestyle—and by doing so, replace meaningless sweatshop and bureaucratic drudgery with real work and more leisure time.

*AMBIGUS*TABILITY: THE SIX FORMS OF WEALTH

Throughout the course of human history, human beings have defined and managed wealth in many ways. In an economic sense, wealth is anything that has utility and is capable of being appropriated or exchanged. In other words, wealth is all those raw resources, refined products, and services that can be used to satisfy our basic needs and excess wants, and that can be traded for other resources, products, and services.

AmbiguStability of Wealth

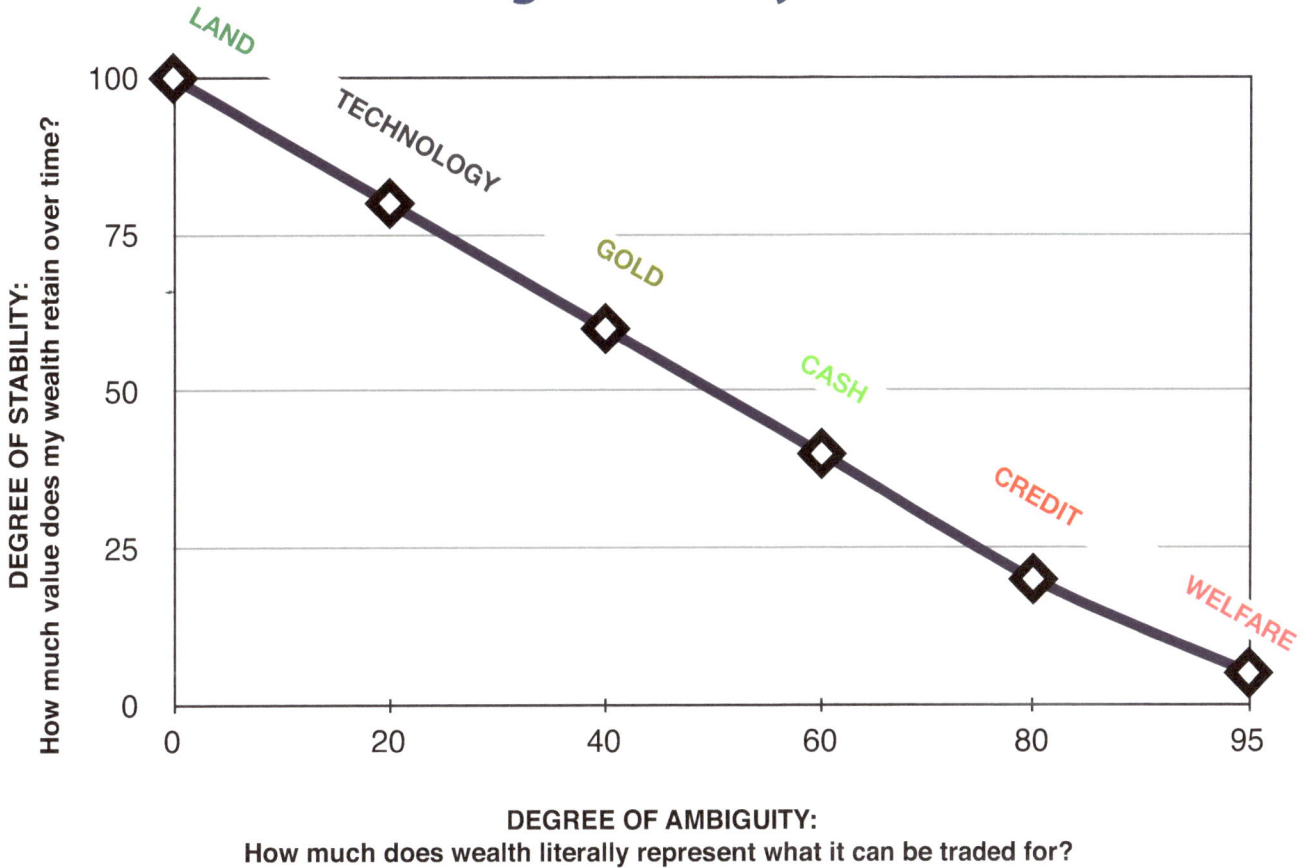

The six major forms of wealth throughout the course of human history have been land, technology, gold, cash, credit, and welfare.

In simple economic systems, such as hunting and gathering and subsistence farming, wealth is most often represented by land, food, and simple tools that are either directly consumed by or traded among individuals, tribes, or nations. As industrialization allowed and encouraged people to migrate farther and faster across the globe, trade grew more complicated. Direct bartering—that is, trading one thing for another—was no longer practical. Coins, which are much easier to transport between trade locations than a pig or a cow, began to represent the exchange value of products and services. Eventually, banking systems cropped up out of the need to store and manage this new form of symbolic wealth. As the banking system grew, so did the need to regulate wealth. Silver, and later gold, began to "back up" monetary wealth. All coinage and cash circulating within an economy were supposedly equivalent to the amount of gold available for their exchange. Credit cards emerged in the twentieth century, allowing customers to charge their purchases with the option to pay back debts over time. Welfare, or charity, has existed throughout time across the globe. In earlier ages, churches were the main providers of charity. Later, certain liberal governments began to share the responsibility with their religious counterparts. Welfare can be donated in the form of money, products, services, and public works projects that are intended to create jobs.

Although all six forms of wealth hold value, they are not equally reliable or accessible to all members of a community or nation. In other words, wealth is only as good as what it can be traded for. Land and technology, the very foundations of our survival, are the most stable forms of wealth. They retain their value over time, both in usability and exchangeability, and they literally represent what they can be traded for. For example, five acres of land and four tractors can almost always be exchanged for land and equipment of equal quality. Land and technology are the least ambiguous forms of wealth. Silver and gold, due to their rarity, beauty, and visual distinguishability, were chosen to represent the amount of currency in circulation within and between nations. Because these metals simultaneously represent tangible wealth (e.g., in the form of jewelry and art) and symbolic wealth, they are less stable than land and technology, but more stable than cash, credit, and welfare, which are purely symbolic forms of wealth. While most merchants will accept cash payments, credit is only accepted if one has a stable credit history. Welfare and other forms of charity, whose recipients remain at the mercy of their benefactors, hold the least power of exchangeability for essential and luxury goods and services.

*Ambigu*Stability is the theory that the more ambiguous, or symbolic, the form of wealth is, the less value it retains over time. Gold and silver coins are more or less obsolete today. Paper currencies lose value due to inflation. Credit cards have maximum balances. Welfare benefits get cut by political and religious authorities. But well-maintained land and technologies never lose their value, since they are the very means of our physical survival.

DISTRIBUTION OF THE SIX FORMS OF WEALTH

Feudalistic, early capitalistic, industrial capitalistic, and ironically, communistic economic systems all share in common an unequal distribution of wealth. For thousands of years, royalty, nobility, landlords, religious authorities, and business elites controlled a majority of the lands, technologies, gold reserves, and currency despite representing only a small minority of the national and world populations. The poor majority slaved away in perpetual indebtedness to their financial superiors—many relying on low pay, credit cards, and religious or government welfare programs to put food on the table. Still countless others face hardships of famine and disease without adequate food and medical care.

Another problem with the more ambiguous, less stable forms of wealth such as cash and credit occurs when consumers lose sight of their true value of attaining goods and services essential for survival and begin to equate financial wealth with social prestige. When this happens, prestige-driven consumers indulge in an excess of luxuries—the production of which often reeks havoc on exploited labor and the natural environment.

Nonetheless, all forms of wealth have their function and place within businesses and economic systems. Cash and credit cards are convenient ways to trade goods and services, while welfare feeds, clothes, and houses those individuals in immediate need. When these forms of wealth are utilized in a logical and balanced manner, they can add much convenience and stability to our economic lives. However, many abuses of these forms of wealth have occurred throughout human history. Thievery, bribery, extortion, embezzlement, credit card scandal, welfare fraud, identity theft, check forgery, unfair labor wages, and money-counterfeit are rampantly taking place in every town, city, and nation across the world.

Although Project Integrity International will integrate all forms of wealth to create and expand as an economic system, it will attempt to safeguard against all kinds of abuses happening within the current economic system. PII, by its very structure, will also serve to redistribute all forms of wealth more evenly between PII participants and non-participants alike.

THE MYTH OF MONEY

As PII strengthens and expands, a great realization will sweep across the collective consciousness of participants across the world. A great and dangerous myth has been plaguing the consciousness and reality of human beings across centuries and continents. This is the myth of money! The myth, that is, that money truly represents what it can be traded for. Every citizen in every country in the world has suffered to some extent from government budgetary cuts that have sacrificed health care, education, and other essential public resources. The more corrupt the government, the less control the citizenry has over the use of its very own taxes. Hard working people more often than not go without health care, adequate education, and most tragically, food, water, and shelter. When budgetary cuts eliminate jobs, able-bodied, eager-to-work laborers are not only barred from earning a living, but are prevented from being producers in their local, national, and global economies. Think about it! If labor is willing and able to work, but the government says "there is no budget to employ them," and the laborers work anyway and still produce product, even without pay, it proves that money did not really represent the labor nor the necessary means of production. In realizing this, we become free to expand and distribute resources without the restriction of "no budget." As PII internalizes a new and powerful economy whereby resources, energy, labor, knowledge, and "money" remain safely within its own system, the flow of wealth will steadily escape from the greedy clutches of corrupt governments and corporations and into the hands of the people. With this critical shift, the people—not the government nor the labor-exploiting corporations—will determine the budget, their economic fates, and the quality of their own lives.

MAPS OF CHANGE

Maps of Change plots out the twelve FOUNDATIONS necessary to satisfy the Six Universal Concerns of human existence. The main objective of Maps of Change is to reveal where WISR Franchises are demanded, permitted, and needed, preventing both scarcity and redundancy of WISR Franchise storefronts in any given locality. Maps of Change are drawn up by a team of expert cartographers, geographers, and statisticians who work in collaboration to continually revise and update the maps for present and future reference.

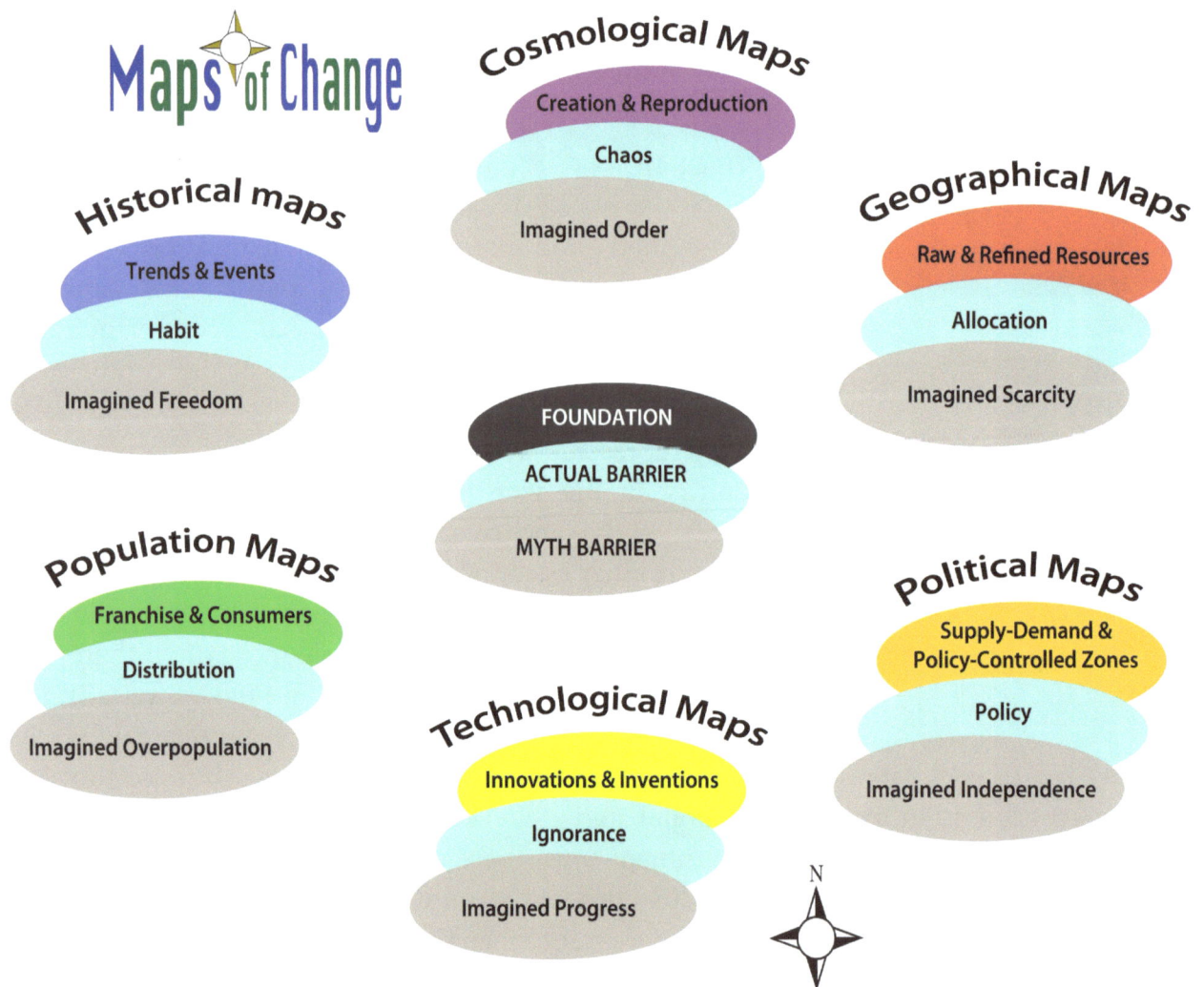

Maps of Change

Cosmological Maps
- Creation & Reproduction
- Chaos
- Imagined Order

Historical maps
- Trends & Events
- Habit
- Imagined Freedom

Geographical Maps
- Raw & Refined Resources
- Allocation
- Imagined Scarcity

FOUNDATION
ACTUAL BARRIER
MYTH BARRIER

Population Maps
- Franchise & Consumers
- Distribution
- Imagined Overpopulation

Technological Maps
- Innovations & Inventions
- Ignorance
- Imagined Progress

Political Maps
- Supply-Demand & Policy-Controlled Zones
- Policy
- Imagined Independence

Maps of Change begins with a thorough examination of both the perceived false "myth barriers" and true "actual barriers" to making positive changes within our communities and environments. Myth barriers are popular false beliefs and ideas that barricade human beings from solving problems and improving their world. Actual barriers are the actual causes of the problems facing human beings. Widely held myths about our environments and world blind us to what is really going on, and thus, inhibit our motivation and ability to effectively address our problems.

Geographical Maps plot out the raw and refined resources available across the globe to satisfy the critical basic needs of healthy air, clean water, nutritious food, and climate-appropriate clothing. One set of maps examines where the world's food can be "cultivated, commodified, consumed, and composted" effectively and affordably. A second set of maps traces both clean air and contaminated air, revealing where restoration and anti-pollution measures must be taken to provide breathable air for humans and ecosystem. Geographical Maps dispel the myth-barrier of scarcity, or the belief that the world has a shortage of vital resources with which to feed, clothe, and house the world's population. Geographical Maps proves that the world has more than enough resources to feed, clothe, and house all human beings. By revealing that the true barrier—misallocation of resources—is the root cause of human starvation and malnutrition, Geographical Maps restores hope to the very people who will utilize the maps to manifest abundance in their communities and beyond.

Political Maps plot out both the supply-demand determined zones and the politically controlled zones within all types of governments that will prove inviting or inhibitive to the establishment and success of WISR Franchises. Political Maps dispel the myth of independence as pedaled by the propagandist mechanisms of so-called democratic states, pop culture, and mainstream media. By shedding light on oppressive and obsolete policies—the root cause of political, cultural, and economic stagnation—Political Maps plot out zones where WISR Franchises will be both demanded by consumers and permitted by the written laws and cultural mores of any given locality.

Technological Maps plot out the innovations and inventions available across the globe necessary to satisfy the critical need of sturdy, safe, and affordable housing, transportation, agricultural tools, textiles, fuels, and other critical technologies. A series of maps examines and pinpoints not only where housing, transportation, and other critical technologies are needed, but what kinds of structures make sense in differing geographical, economic, and cultural "climates"; where the current industries are growing or stagnating; and where alternative, more effective innovations are being popularized. Technological Maps dispel the myth of technological progress—or the illusion that technological advancement is the greatest measure of human success. Rather, Technological Maps proves that the true barrier—technological ignorance characterized by misuse, overuse, and unnecessary production of needless, harmful technologies—is the root cause of environmental pollution and human injury. Technological Maps plot out the path to the next wave of industrialization that is designed to preserve the natural environment, maintain human safety, and provide vital necessities.

Population Maps plot out the franchisees and consumers available across the globe that are interested in owning and patronizing WISR Franchises. By knowing where WISR Franchises will be permitted, accepted, and patronized by local target markets, time, money, resources, and energy will not be foolishly squandered where franchises do not prove popular or profitable. Population Maps dispels the myth of overpopulation, that is, that there are too many people to sustainably support. On the contrary, Population Maps proves that the true barrier—maldistribution of population as caused by poor communication systems and ineffective community layout—is the root cause of unemployment and underemployment. Population Maps plot out where community restoration efforts must take place for the effective functioning of WISR Franchises.

Historical Maps plot out past and present economic trends and events that foster or inhibit healthy economic growth throughout the world. Tracking political, cultural, and economic phenomena, these maps reveal where and why ineffective, unhealthy, and stagnant circumstances happen to individuals, communities, and nations. Historical Maps dispel the myth of freedom—which is enjoyed by a privileged few and denied to many. Conversely, Historical Maps argues that the true barrier—maladaptive personal and collective habits as learned from ignorant parenting strategies, stale education systems, and popular media—is the root cause of repeating unhealthy trends. Historical Maps plot the path to an innovative educational framework necessary to continually maintain and enhance cultural, political, and economic systems to be utilized by present and future generations.

Cosmological Maps, by examining "energy into matter" processes, plot out the current creation and reproduction processes dominating major industries across the globe. By analyzing and understanding how factories, laboratories, and other types of production facilities operate, these maps will allow us to model effective production methods that benefit WISR Franchisees and consumers while rejecting those that prove useless, obsolete, or injurious. Cosmological Maps dispels the myth of order—which is little more than an illusion produced by neat rows of assembly line workers. Conversely, Cosmological Maps reveal the actual barrier—the chaotic mayhem characterizing many factory plants that lead to pollution, waste, and a general sense of meaningless on the job. Cosmological Maps will lay the foundation for safe, meaningful production and distribution of WISR brand products and services.

Maps of Change will not only be used by expert scientists and business administrators participating in Project Integrity International, but will be presented as educational tools for all visitors to PII's website.

PII BUSINESS PLAN

PII'S BUSINESS STRUCTURE

Critical to the success of PII is financial accessibility of franchise opportunities to all interested participants. The start-up costs of the average franchise exceed the expendable income of many low- and middle class individuals. Therefore, PII will incorporate a loan, scholarship, and grant program to assist franchise prospects to afford the training and intern program tuition fees as well as the start-up and ongoing expenses of their franchises.

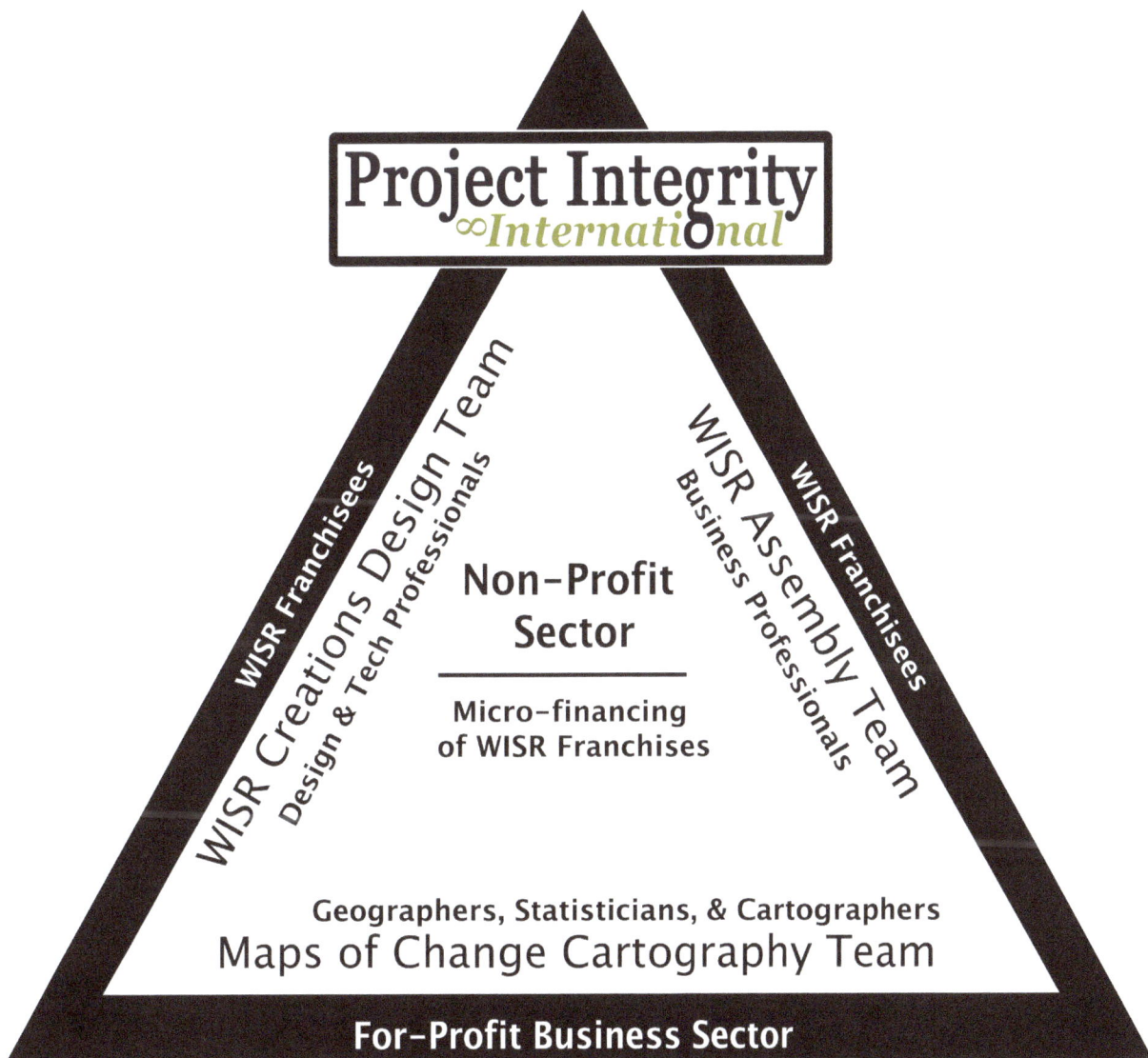

Project Integrity ∞International

WISR Franchisees
WISR Creations Design Team
Design & Tech Professionals

WISR Franchisees
WISR Assembly Team
Business Professionals

Non-Profit
Sector

Micro-financing
of WISR Franchises

Geographers, Statisticians, & Cartographers
Maps of Change Cartography Team

For-Profit Business Sector

PII will start out by inviting interested participants to an online forum where they can create their own unique Network Profile Page and begin to collaborate with others. Profits generated by the PII Online Networking Forum's extensive ad campaign and featured services will be rolled into funds for the initial non-profit sector think tanks of WISR Assembly, WISR Creations, and Maps of Change Cartography Center. Both salaried experts and volunteers will design the prototypes for PII's businesses, products, and services. In turn, profits will be generated by selling products and services to existing storefronts across the globe. These profits will later serve to provide the scholarships, loans, and grants for future franchisees. The constant cycling of funds will serve not only to aid and abet the growth of PII's business establishments, but to continually improve the quality of WISR products and services.

PII'S RELATIONSHIP WITH OTHER BUSINESS ENTITIES

PII's relationship with other business entities throughout PII's market zones will be friendly, fair, and symbiotic. Out of respect for established businesses, PII will cooperate with other business entities to foster growth, independence, and abundance for all parties involved.

Small Businesses	**Conversion**—PII will assist other small businesses who wish to become more sustainable while remaining independent; alternatively, small businesses have the option to convert to WISR Franchises.
Independent Green Businesses	**Collaboration**—PII will shelve other green brands, thus boosting profits and market exposure; also, PII welcomes green businesses who wish to convert into WISR Franchises.
Fortune 500s & Franchises	**Competition**—PII considers the "big guys" fair competition. Let's play!
Academia	**Affiliation**—PII will recruit experts, intellectuals, artists, and students from public, private, and alternative educational facilities from all corners of the world and create empowering affiliations with other academic facilities.
Non–Profits	**Cooperation**—PII will work with non-profits to make WISR franchising a more viable opportunity in low income neighborhoods, cities, and nations.

PII will assist other small businesses who wish to become more sustainable while remaining independent. Small businesses will also have the option to convert to a WISR Franchise, taking advantage of their brand identity to strengthen their product's or service's popularity. PII will shelve the products of existing green businesses, thus boosting their profits and market exposure. When it comes to Fortune 500s, multinationals, and other franchises, PII considers the "big guys" fair competition. Let's play! PII will recruit experts, artists, and students from public, private, and alternative educational facilities from all corners of the world and create empowering affiliations with other schools. Finally, PII will work with non-profits to make the WISR Franchise more viable opportunities in poor neighborhoods, cities, and nations.

By not threatening established businesses, PII will maintain harmony between all individuals within its market zones while improving the world's cultural, environmental, and economic climate.

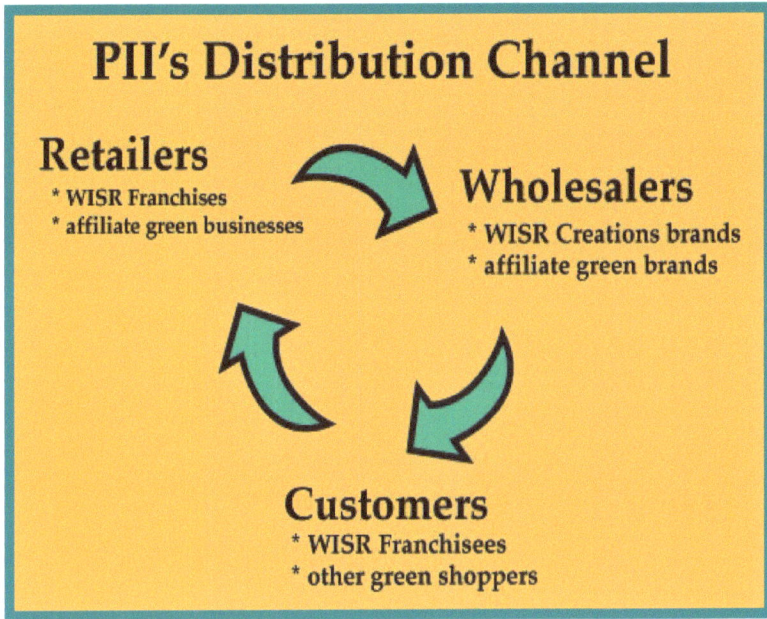

PII's Distribution Channel

Retailers
* WISR Franchises
* affiliate green businesses

Wholesalers
* WISR Creations brands
* affiliate green brands

Customers
* WISR Franchisees
* other green shoppers

Bureaucratic Waste: PII vs. Non-Profits

PII Model

Non-Profits Model

⚬ : "white collar" administrators depleting time and funds otherwise spent on producing real products and services

⚬ : "blue collar" labor producing real products and services

PII'S DISTRIBUTION CHANNEL

PII serves to bridge green business retailers, wholesalers, and consumers who choose to utilize PII's distribution channel to sell and buy sustainable products and services. WISR stores' shelves will not only be stocked with WISR brands, but will carry other green brands who will benefit from increased profits and market exposure. Conversely, independent green retail outlets will also increase profits through the sale of popular WISR brand products that they select to stock on their own shelves. Environmentally conscious consumers will enjoy the convenience of being able to purchase their favorite WISR and other green brands from both WISR franchises and other green stores. Internet shopping sites will also prove invaluable distribution channels for both WISR and other green brands. PII's inviting, all-encompassing, far-reaching distribution channels will not only serve to bring healthy resources and products to all corners of the earth, but will spread the word of PII's franchise opportunities to millions of people who seek more promising livelihoods.

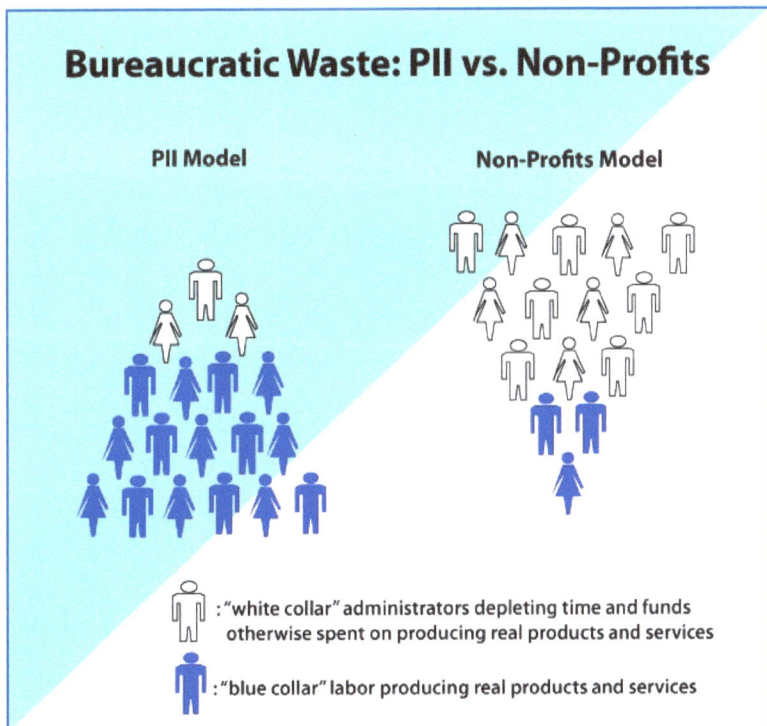

PII HEADQUARTERS

Although economic policies vary within and between nations, all countries, states, and cities across the world have legal regulations over all business entities. WISR Franchises, as an international chain, must meet the economic regulations, codes, and policies at municipal, state, and federal levels of jurisdiction. Because many franchisees participating in PII will not have business educations, knowledge, and know-how, PII provides the team of experts and professionals to provide assistance with administrative tasks.

Importantly, because franchise businesses use uniform training manuals and other legal documents, PII will drastically cut costly administration needs, and thus, avoid getting caught in sticky red tape that trap so many entrepreneurs. Project Integrity International Headquarters branches will exist in convenient, central locations throughout PII's market zones across the world.

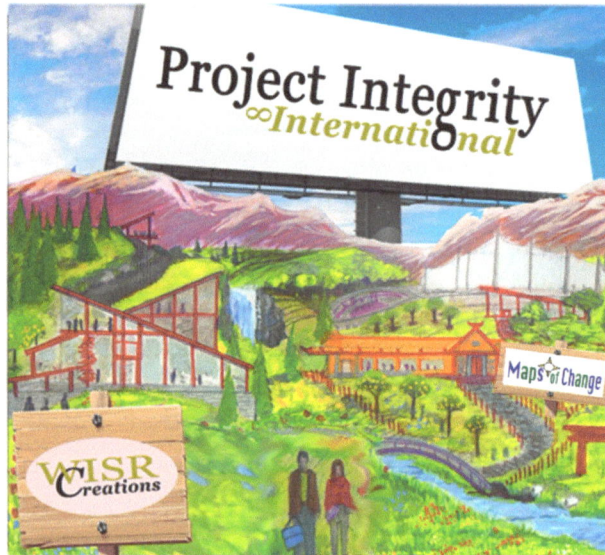

WISR ASSEMBLY

WISR Assembly team members will work both at PII Headquarters and out in the field. WISR Assembly is made up of nine units, each set up, operated, and maintained by team members.

While individual franchisees do their own accounting, file their own taxes, and track their own cash flow, the **WISR Accounting** team provides assistance with and training for WISR Franchisees that are unskilled at such tasks. WISR Accounting also deals with the flow of capital and owner stocks for the larger PII establishment.

WISR Realty is a team of real estate agents that procure the land and property where WISR Franchises will be opened and operated. In addition, WISR real estate professionals will be available to assist franchisees with the purchasing and refinancing of their personal property.

WISR Insurance is a team of insurance brokers that will ensure that all franchises hold the right kinds of insurance policies legally required to protect franchisees and their clients in the case of accidents, lawsuits, and natural disasters.

WISR Marketing is a team of marketers and advertisers who will devise and implement effective promotional plans for popularizing WISR products and services; design television, radio, internet, and print ads; and conduct the market research necessary to make WISR Franchises a success.

Maps of Change consists of a team of expert geographers, cartographers, researchers, and statisticians who design and continually update and archive a series of maps that will be used to plot out where WISR Franchises will be demanded, permitted, and patronized.

WISR Training is a team of educators who will teach, train, and coach future franchisees how to most effectively operate their businesses. All aspects of owning and operating a business will be taught, such as accounting, bookkeeping, customer service skills, advertising, and human resources.

WISR Law is a team of attorneys who will take care of the legal aspects of both PII and individual franchises, such as acquiring business licenses, incorporation processes, and other legal aspects of owning and operating businesses.

WISR Technical, a team of engineers, computer tech specialists, web developers, and other technological experts who assist PII's franchisees with all the technical aspects of owning and operating their businesses.

Although PII is structured to ensure fairness and harmony between franchisees, costumers, and others, interpersonal problems are inevitable. **WISR Mediation** is a team of conflict resolution mediators who will provide counseling services for franchisees who are experiencing difficulties in their professional relationships.

In addition to the nine teams of PII, external bankers and investors will manage and precipitate money transfer, loans, and grants. The nine teams of WISR Assembly will work separately and together to help franchisees make the most of their businesses, and thus, make PII a success.

WISR CREATIONS: GLOBAL BRAND, LOCAL FLAVOR.

WISR Creations is the "laboratories" where the prototypes for future WISR Franchises products and services will be conceptualized, designed, produced, and enhanced. WISR Creations team consists of experts, technicians, scientists, engineers, architects, artists, innovators, and contractors who take on the responsibility for conceptualizing, designing, creating, and enhancing the initial prototypical products and services to be produced, distributed, and sold at WISR Franchises. All members will hold shares of WISR Creations.

PII's Maps of Change team of cartographers strategically market products and services to global areas that both need and demand the products, thus avoiding over- and underproduction.

WISR Creations' motto is "Global Brand, Local Flavor." Unlike most global franchise chains, no two WISR Franchises will be the same. Although all franchises will distribute and sell WISR Creations retail products, franchisees will design and decorate their storefronts, market their products, and present themselves to the public in a way that is unique to their own personalities and cultural backgrounds. For example, all WISR brand restaurants will use the same high-quality, organic, fair-trade ingredients in their cuisine, but their individual menus will reflect the talents, preferences, and cultural backgrounds of individual WISR Franchisees. Like the greater natural environment, WISR Franchisees will celebrate endless, mind-inspiring diversity.

WISR CREATIONS: SIX SUBSIDIARIES OF PII

WISR Creations is a diversified corporation of six main subsidiaries operating internationally and across the globe.

WISR Nourish is a subsidiary of WISR Creations that deals with both "the four C's" of food production"—cultivation, commodification, consumption, and composting—as well as air and water pollution restoration processes. Products will include not only food and air restoration goods and services, but also the equipment needed to grow, prepare, distribute, and sell the products. A WISR Franchisee may choose to open up a produce stand, a garden supplies shop, a café/ restaurant, a health food store, an air or water purifier distribution center, a green house, or an organic farm. When conducting trade with independent farmers, vegetation and meats will meet certified organic, fair-trade, and "freshness" standards.

WISR Entertainments is a subsidiary of WISR Creations that provides healthy, enjoyable sources of entertainment that simultaneously promote mental, physical, and spiritual growth, creativity—and having a great time! A WISR Franchisee may choose to open up a music supplies shop, a sporting goods store, an activity-specific learning center, a dance club, a sound recording studio, a theater, video gaming arcade, or other entertainment facility.

WISR Designs is a subsidiary of WISR Creations that provides adequate, effective, and safe housing, transportation, textiles, and other technologies essential for human survival and comfort. A WISR Franchisee may choose to open up an alternative fuel station, a natural clothing production facility, an alternative housing production plant, a chemistry lab, or any retail store which sells WISR Creation's technological products and services.

WISR Communications is a subsidiary of WISR Creations that provides both non-technological and technological communication solutions that harmoniously connect individuals and communities across the globe. Examples of WISR Franchises which are designed to produce and distribute non-technological communication solutions include foreign language tutorial centers, Braille and foreign language translator services, publishing companies, book stores, and magazines. Examples of technological communications co-ops include companies that create, manufacture, repair, and sell computer hardware/software, telephones, internet, and private-sector postal mail services.

WISR Learning WISR Learning is an educational facility that not only provides exercise of the mind, body, and spirit, but prepares students for the many roles and tasks of operating WISR Franchises. "WISR" is an acronym standing for Wave Image Symbol Reality, and is a theory which views the human experience as being made of three "mental modes" of existence. The quality of one's "Reality" is determined by the inter-functioning of these mental modes.

The first mode we experience in the WISR cycle is the WaveState, which involves our INTUITIVE self responsible for "gut knowing," emotional experience, and even extrasensory perception. The second mode we experience is the ImageState, which involves our IMAGINATIVE self as experienced through seeing, hearing, tasting, touching, and smelling the world. The third mode we experience is the SymbolState, which involves our INTELLECTUAL self responsible for using letters, numbers, and other symbol sets to come to (and record!) a rational understanding of ourselves and our environments. Finally, when the three modes—Intuition, Imagination, and Intelligence—are harmonized within the individual, she or he enjoys a state of ILLUMINATION—elevated self-esteem, confidence, ability, spontaneity, and passion for life!

By setting up, running, and maintaining WISR Learning centers throughout the world, a team of expert-instructors in the age-appropriated activities offered provide the education necessary to bring about the success of Project Integrity International.

WISR Learning elementary, high school, adult, and collegiate level activities are offered as both an after-school program and as individual evening and weekend classes for participants of all ages. The numerous activities offered are not only life-applicable and entertaining, but foster one's emotional, physical, and intellectual awareness and development. Based on WISR Theory's "Map of The Mind," the activities engage the part of the brain responsible for executing the activity task at hand. Classes are conducted in a unique, innovative way that leaves each WISR Learning participant with a whole new set of skills and a newfound balance between mind, body, and spirit.

WISR Learning elementary, high School, and adult level activities include twelve subjects necessary for the effective establishment of WISR Franchises.

"Computers," "Business," "Numbers," "Words," and "Building & Design" prepare participants to innovate and invent the endless products and services to be sold on the shelves of all WISR storefronts. Participants will design and sew clothing, plant and maintain gardens, and design and build housing, transportation, bridges, and other technologies. With the basics of "Words" and "Numbers" down, students will use their basic grammatical and mathematical skills to plan and eventually—run!—their very own businesses. Here, they will write a resume, bio, and business plan; balance a checkbook; and learn all other business basics. Participants graduate prepared to open a business of their own. A strong emphasis will be placed on all aspects of the essential art of computer literacy.

"Meditation", "Yoga", and "Healing Arts & Nutrition" courses will prepare the future healers that will open up WISR Healing and WISR Nourish franchise branches. Participants are instructed in the art of both western and eastern healing methods. A dual emphasis on prevention and cure leads participants down the path to leading healthier lives. A wide array of topics and activities will be discussed and explored, such as nutrition, yoga, therapy, medicine, constructive thinking, visualization, and more.

"Defense Arts", "Music", "Arts", and "Dance" will enrich participants' intellectual, emotional, physical, and spiritual lives with endless awe-inspiring lessons while preparing those individuals who will establish future WISR Entertainment franchises.

WISR Learning collegiate level activities—Humanities, Sciences, Economics, and Athletics —engage participants in the theoretical aspects of all fields explored and applied by the greater PII establishment. During Humanities instruction, participants explore anthropological, psychological, sociological, philosophical, and linguistic assessments of our world, while utilizing research findings to improve the quality of life between and within all life species and ecosystems. During Sciences instruction, participants explore biology, psychiatry, medicine, chemistry, geology, geography, and physics while devising practical applications of their inventions and discoveries. Economics instruction involves participants in critically examining world economic systems, why they succeed or fail, and how they may be improved upon. Athletics instruction engages "the mind in thinking about the body." During instruction, participants learn about, design, and engage in sports, body movement, and other forms of physical expression. Through fun exploration and stimulating experimentation, participants learn how to physically stay fit, healthy—and entertained! Importantly, WISR collegiate level participants will lead the way to continual improvement of WISR Franchises across the globe.

WISR Healing centers, dispersed throughout PII's market zones, will provide affordable therapy plans tailored to the unique healing needs of individuals and communities. WISR Healing utilizes many traditional and modern healing techniques in conjunction to address the many various health problems affecting individuals and communities. Psychotherapists, massage therapists, surgeons, herbalists, psychiatrists, psychics, and other healers of both Eastern and Western traditions will open WISR Franchise healing centers across the globe.

WISR FRANCHISES

WISR Franchises simultaneously promote business efficacy, efficiency, and equality. As a franchise, WISR Franchises can maximize efficacy by spreading far and fast across nations and continents. Two features unique to franchise businesses that foster their rapid growth are their brand name familiarity to consumers who seek pre-assured high quality; and their popularity as achieved through wide-scale advertising and word-of-mouth. As sustainable businesses, WISR Franchises place strong emphasis on providing goods and services that foster environmental and human health. In doing so, WISR Franchises maximize efficiency by minimizing wasteful production procedures and discouraging addictive consumer habits. Finally, as co-ops, WISR Franchisees will enjoy equal access to profit earning, skill-building, and decision-making opportunities.

In addition to earning profits generated by their franchise businesses, franchisees will be issued shares in the greater PII establishment. The WISR Franchise opportunity is open to persons of all ages, races, nationalities, sexual orientations, professions, and genders who successfully complete the WISR Franchise application, training, and intern program.

WISR CLUSTER

A WISR Cluster consists of a varietal group of WISR Creation subsidiaries and WISR Franchises that work interdependently to satisfy the Six Universal Concerns of any given locality. Using Maps of Change, franchises are strategically located to avoid scarcity or redundancy of goods and services, thus ensuring maximal satiation of needs and minimal waste in any given area. Further, by eliminating excessive competition between like co-ops, all participants can more effectively cooperate to bring abundance, balance, and harmony to their communities and beyond. Participants are encouraged to "close the economy" by purchasing products and services from WISR Franchises rather than other existing businesses. Greater profit shares, high product quality, lower prices, and WISR member discount plans will serve as incentives to this end.

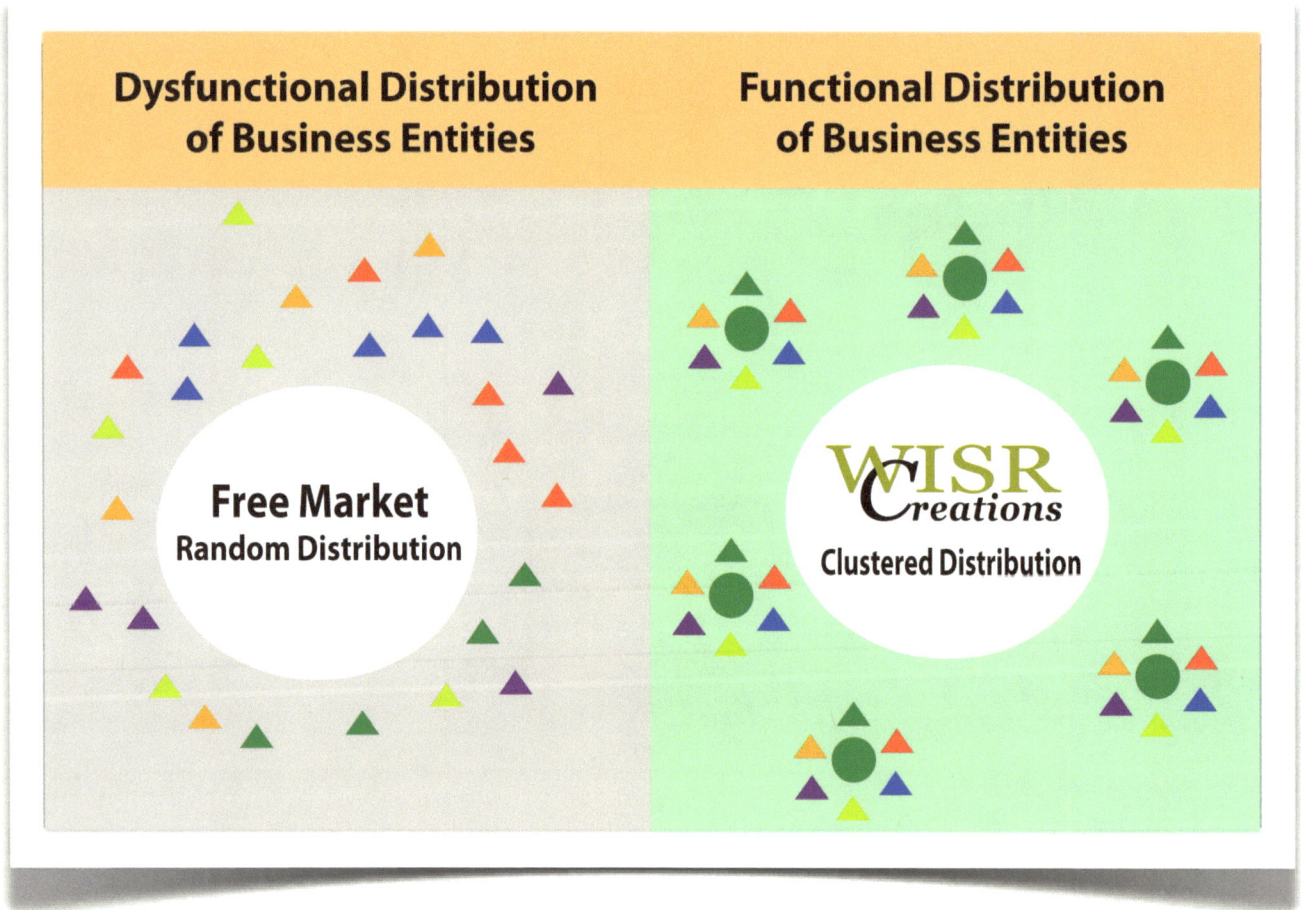

PII VS. GREEN MARKET CAPITALISM

Under free market capitalism, green businesses are privy to the same obstacles as conventional ones. Because green entrepreneurs choose locations for their businesses based solely on their own circumstances and economic goals, they relinquish control over their immediate surroundings.

For example, a health food store operating under free market capitalism has no say over what type or how many businesses open within its market zone. A health food store may end up neighboring a toxic factory or other groceries that encroach on their clientele base.

On the contrary, WISR Franchises are strategically positioned to provide maximum profit potential and healthy surroundings. Like popular chain stores such as Starbucks, Burger King, and Wendy's, WISR will expand its market zones through mass popularization of its brand name products and services, and thus, increase its store location options throughout the world. While WISR creates a close-knit community whereby all franchisees play the roles of owner, shareholder, and client, random green business owners often remain isolated from each other and operate under traditional hierarchical structures that limit individual potential. Without this community of support that keeps resources and profits circulating within, independent green businesses are more likely to fail, and thus, dissipate their wealth back into the toxic, conventional business establishments that buy them out.

ROLE-TATION: WORKER/OWNER/SHAREHOLDER/CLIENT

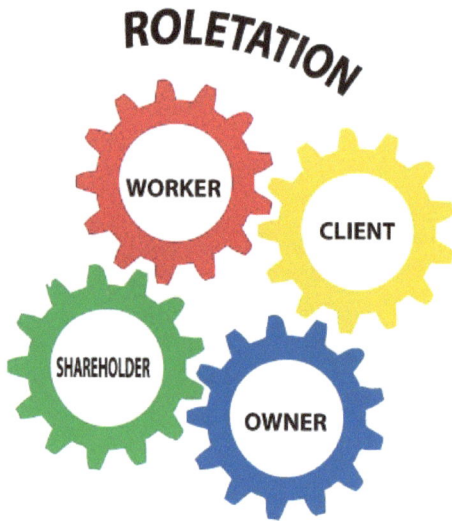

The success of WISR Franchises will be determined by the individual and collective effort on the part of all franchisees involved. As discussed above, the four roles that all franchisees will play are that of worker, owner, shareholder, and client. WISR Franchises, by definition, are owned in equal part by each co-owner. As workers, franchise co-op members will pitch in to complete all tasks involved, such as accounting, product production, clean-up, customer service, stocking, and inventory. By "role-tating" through various tasks, all franchisees develop a variety of necessary skills and talents. Thus, franchisees avoid getting trapped in the monotony of traditional business models that keep people in rigid roles, such as janitors who do all the cleaning and accountants who do all the financial figuring. As franchise owners and shareholders, entrepreneurs not only earn profits generated by their private businesses, but own profit shares of Project Integrity International. Therefore, the more co-op franchises that form and succeed, the greater the profit shares for each franchisee and the stronger the foundation for present and future success for all participants involved. Finally, as WISR Creations Stores' clients and customers, franchisees will cycle their profits back into PII's market economy, strengthening the system for all participants. Hence, PII participants are granted the opportunity for continual intellectual, emotional, physical, economic, and spiritual success.

CO-OPETITION: COOPERATION WITHIN COMPETITION

While our present economy is characterized by a dog-eat-dog approach that too often leaves many people without adequate jobs, resources, and education, PII incorporates an approach that fosters sufficient entrepreneurial opportunities, education, and resource accessibility for all franchisees. Although PII promotes healthy cooperation within and between co-op franchises, it also fosters, employs, and celebrates the inborn human instinct of competition. Friendly competition between co-op franchises encourages and motivates franchisees to continually improve their businesses, customer relations, and communities. Like sports and games, friendly competition will prove to be an endless source of fun, excitement, and inspiration to keep both franchisees and other PII participants progressing towards their personal and collective goals.

SPECIAL SOURCES

Although Project Integrity International creates and promotes a cleaner world, our current world is chockfull of danger zones. Nuclear power plants, endless landfills, depleted rain-forests, contaminated lands, and polluted waterways are just a few such examples. Special Sources is a team of experts, technicians, scientists, clean-up crew members, and other environmental restoration authorities who will work to clean up existing danger zones throughout the world—and set the stage for a future that avoids their manifestation.

WISR NETWORKS

As WISR Franchises grow in number across the globe by occupying and accruing both commercial and residential real estate properties, participants will increasingly have the option to live closer to their own storefronts. Eventually, the WISR Franchise unit will merge with participants' residential quarters, together comprising a **WISR Network** that can be built and installed into the community from the get-go.

WISR Networks are a collective living area where basic needs are produced and consumed "in one's own backyard," therefore reducing waste of energy, time, space, resources, and labor otherwise spent distributing products across great distances. WISR Networks are communities whereby individuals grow their own food, sew their own clothes, build their own homes, educate their own children, run their own businesses, and celebrate their own lives. Therefore, each Network is uniquely designed by its inhabitants according to their own needs and preferences. Although no two Networks will be alike in style, all will share the common goals of producing basic needs for their inhabitants, maintaining peace both within and between Networks, and nurturance of the shared greater natural environment.

As local Networks grow in number across the world, the existence of large, often toxic factories will diminish along with the need for them. With this shift, participants will begin to restore the natural environment while providing for their basic needs locally and sustainably.

CONCLUSION: An Invitation to All

Project Integrity International's main task is to maintain and improve the new global system for present and future generations.

PII will strive to strike balanced relationships between individuals and the collective, education and entertainment, work and play, economy and environment, and competition and cooperation.

Welcoming individuals from all walks of life, PII will transform the world into a place where all will come to celebrate universal similarities as well as beautiful differences.

Every individual will be afforded access to each of the Six Universal Concerns of Humankind by playing a direct role in innovating, producing, and providing the goods and services necessary to meet individual and community needs. Further, every individual will share the opportunity to dynamically participate in a variety of roles and tasks of PII, and thus, joyously exercise all aspects of their minds, bodies, and spirits.

By respecting the autonomy of each individual, PII will create and promote a general feeling of connectedness within and between co-ops and communities.

Self-willing participants will work to dismantle the weaponry of yesterday and assemble the tools of today. Gardens will replace nuclear facilities and parks will replace unnecessary strip malls as fresh air blows away the stagnation of a polluted yesterday.

Project Integrity is not a Fantasy of Utopia, but rather a Reality of Perpetual Progress. Problems will arise, but so will the people to address and solve them in the most strategically and compassionately agreed upon way.

PII welcomes you, PII welcomes all.

∞

Project Integrity International

Owners of the world, unite!

∞

owners of the world, unite
don't give up
without an entrepreneurial fight

engineers of the world, unite
design us a more efficient technology
which fosters our economy
and preserves our ecology

architects of the world, unite
draft a sustainable home
strength of a geodesic dome
that withstands earthquakes,
hurricanes and tornados
shielding us from head to toe
and all of life's great big woes

farmers of the world, unite
and grow us some carrots and potatoes
practice pristine permaculture
bring together the Eagle, Crane, and Vulture

nutritionists of the world, unite
design us a diet to end obesity's plight
psychologists of the world, unite
and heal our collective mental plight
biologists of the world, unite
jettison genetic engineering's blight

women of the world, unite
and go with your gut feelings
make an iron fist
and smash open the glass ceiling
children of the world, unite
and quit taking parental abuse

55

let your parents know
that there ain't no excuse

teachers of the world, unite
and show us how to do it
experts of the world, unite
and show us how to execute it

now I stated the problem
now I'm offering a solution
it's a revolution
revolving back
to a forward evolution

the city back into the community
the town back into a tribe
but the tribe modified
by organic technologies
with corporate apologies
for former atrocities

the co-op as base
for the conglomeration
of corporations
a franchise of co-ops
ecosustainably on top!
owned by each
owned by all
equal shares
of one abundant whole
opportunity for each—
opportunity for all!

let us wisen up about our tax bracket
and wrap our assets
in a corporation

one global corporation
a billion local co-operations
profits earned by the many
taxed as merely one

now let us get together
and have some fiscal fun

Project Integrity— incorporated
all wastefulness negated

realtors of the world, unite
and buy us up some land
let us get together
super-size the supply
and determine the demand
let us pool our many fortunes and facets
and sum total our collective assets
lawyers of the world, unite
and help us to incorporate

brokers of the world, unite
and buy shares in our company
let us save the planet
while earning us some money

realtors and brokers,
lawyers and insurers,
unite to help us with this fight
administrate with less red tape
make the great bureaucratic escape
leverage the logistics
keep track of the statistics
for your franchisee sons and daughters
put the team together
at Project Integrity Headquarters
Project Integrity—incorporated
satisfaction guaranteed
or you will be rebated
we promise to return your funds
if you find us overrated

owners of the world, unite
and even up the score
divvy up the profits
as we open WISR Stores

Six Universal Concerns
for which everybody yearns
let us provide these needs
and greatest profits earn

let our corporation diversify
as our many needs vary
one conglomeration
six subsidiaries

WISR Nutrition
one healthy corporation
carrots and cucumbers
more oxygen while we slumber
plant the seeds, rotate the crop
spare the land and grow the numbers

WISR Entertainment—
a medley of music and movies
get your pleasures
at any measure
they will
thrill your mind
and thrill your soul
but most important
they will put the hardy soup
in the party bowl
get down and get groovy
while promoting
ecological sustainment
enjoy **WISR Entertainment!**

WISR Designs
our homes sturdy and fine
geodesically sound
the meaning profound—
efficiency found!
more efficient transportation
the solution is our destination
always on time
the skies are blue

and the air divine!
so come on in
and shop **WISR Designs**

WISR Creations
a world elevated
wastefulness negated
spread the message across all nations
with **WISR Communications**

phones that link our homes
networks to share our poems
did you visit our webpage yet?
on **WISR Internet**?
did you surf the almighty
WISR World Web?

so next time when the commercials
have made you impatient
simply turn that station
to **WISR Communications**!

and when your mind is yearning
for information
come visit us at **WISR Learning**
to indulge in mental fascination
learn the basics to survive
and feel your spirit thrive

but when you're feeling ill
don't just pop a pill
no matter how bad you're feeling
come on in to **WISR Healing**

come explore **WISR Stores**
we won't leave you isolated—
we are strategically located
just the right amount
evenly spread out!
everyone self-employed
lots of time

leisurely enjoyed
come now, let us plot the map
and plan the ploy
let us escape the trap—
let us re-arrange
with Maps of Change

Geographical Maps
plot treasures to be tapped
map the raw resources
which prove very necessary
to put refined products
on the shelves at **WISR Stores**

Political Maps
cut the crap!
let us determine where
supply-demand calls out
where local clients avow
and where local policies allow
for the seeds of **WISR** to sprout

Technological Maps
preserve the ice caps
let us be aware
let us plot with care
inventions which spare the air
and innovations worldwide
which foster ecosustainable pride

Population Maps
escape the tourist trap
let us map public interest
that in **WISR Stores**
wish to invest
let us locate our owners
let us market our consumers
WISR Stores are coming!
go ahead! spread the rumor!

Historical Maps

plot the escape
from yesterday's trap
let us map our past
let us discover
the trends which made us last
and the events that were over fast
which trends should we continue?
which events should we never repeat?
which habits are healthy?
which habits lead to our defeat?

Cosmological Maps

measure the great galactic gap
let us determine
the best way to create
products at an efficient rate
energy into matter
matter into energy
let us master reproduction
with the greatest magnitude of synergy

clever the vision-
WISR the mission!

WISR Creations
or global destruction
the decision is yours
will you close the windows
or open the doors?*

∞

*These song lyrics appear in a dynamic multi-genre hip hop musical movie written and to be produced by the author. More info : www.kangaroofu.com.

ABOUT THE AUTHOR

ABCrane enjoys her work as a socioeconomic visionary who dares to walk the tightrope between fantasy and reality, between the mundane and the surreal, and between truth and illusion. From early childhood, she has been one to question answers and answer questions. A Bachelor's degree in Sociology prepared ABCrane to better analyze the problems of the world while a double major in Creative Writing coached her how to imagine, innovate, invent — and write! — about solutions to those problems. Her other works include *What is Wealth: Thinking Bavk and Moving Forward*, an ecclective series of essays on subjects such as religion economics, and sociology; *Feel Wheel: Emotional Intelligence for the Radical Thinker*; and *Kangaroo Fu: The HipHopera*, an en progress full feature "hip-hopera" musical movie in three acts.

Buy this book, fund the author's new musical!

What better a way to express a serious socioeconomic vision than with singing, dancing, martial arts and an exciting story line! Proceeds generated from the sale of this book will fund the production of the author's new musical, **Kangaroo Fu: The HipHopera.** *Fu* follows the journey of a band of zoo escapees on their way to a paradise that, come to find out, is up to them to create! more: www.projectintegrity.biz and www.kangaroofu.com

www.ingramcontent.com/pod-product-compliance
Lightning Source LLC
Chambersburg PA
CBHW041704200326
41518CB00003B/187